Dining with Friends
The Art of North American Vegan Cuisine

This book is dedicated to each person who is willing to take a chance,

Who stands out as different when indifference is the norm,

And whose main ingredient is love.

Special thanks to Donna Labati-Thigpen, who
supported the writing of this book from its inception.

Table of Contents

Introduction

How Friends of Animals Got Our Recipe

The word *vegetarian* – derived from the Latin *vegetus,* meaning whole, fresh, or lively – was first used in 1847, at the inaugural meeting of the Vegetarian Society in a seaside village known as Ramsgate, in the county of Kent, England. The American Vegetarian society held its inaugural meeting in New York just three years later, in May of 1850, with William Alcott accepting the position of president.

A century later, a new group in England reclaimed an even earlier tradition of maintaining a plant-based diet as part of striving to live a morally consistent life. The term *vegan* (pronounced VEE-gun) was reportedly coined in a 1944 meeting convened by Donald Watson, a conscientious objector later acclaimed as the Vegan Society's founder, and Elsie Shrigley. They created the word from the first and last letters of *vegetarian* because veganism starts with vegetarianism and carries it through to its logical conclusion: dairy-free living. And while *vegetarian* may describe a diet, *vegan* embodies an ethical commitment to live, as far as possible, in harmony with the planet and all its inhabitants.

It took some time for the idea to gain a foothold.

Until the 1970s, people rarely questioned the custom of drinking the milk of other mammals, and the word "vegan" was virtually unheard in North America. Indeed, not one of this book's contributors started out life as a vegan. Today, we know that behind every great mocha latté is a veal calf. Dairy farmers deem male calves useless – except, for example, as future pieces of veal. So every time we look at a piece of cheese in the dairy case, we know it means turning away from a calf. Suddenly, giving up milk stops being difficult and becomes an affirmative act in furtherance of a peaceful culture. And to think that the person who founded our group in 1957 was Alice Herrington – the adopted daughter of Wisconsin dairy farmers!

In December of 2003, *The New York Times* ran an article called "The Homeless and the Meatless: A Deer Hunt to Aid the Hungry Brings a Vegan Response" – an example of Friends of Animals bringing the word "vegan" into major media headlines.[1] When bow-hunters promised the bodies of deer to a Stamford soup kitchen through an initiative called "Hunters for the Hungry" in exchange for being able to hunt with bows on the Audubon Society's Connecticut property, Friends of Animals stepped in to offer vegan meals instead.

"I don't think we have to shoot the state's deer to feed the hungry," said Friends of Animals president Priscilla Feral. The newspaper included Priscilla's recipe for Tempeh London Broil (included under *Enchanting Innovations* in this book's *Main Dishes* section).

It is doubtless true, worldwide, that eating other animals isn't the best response to a hungry society. It's been suggested that for each average eight-ounce steak – with all the grain and costs it represents in total – we could fill the plates of forty-five people eating grains.[2] Furthermore, we know that "improved animal welfare" – more space and resources for other animals who will be eaten – simply cannot work for six billion people in a world of finite resources.

And then there's the planet, slowly ravaged by the pollution in its waters and the intensive use of fossil fuels in animal agriculture. By avoiding products of the deforestation that creates grazing land, observes John Robbins, each vegetarian saves an acre of trees per year, which leaves the other animals on our planet there in their natural habitat. Because trees absorb carbon dioxide, sparing the forests also provides a key to preserving the earth's atmosphere.

Animals in agriculture now outnumber human beings three to one. Already they consume half the world's grain. Soon, as George Monbiot wrote in London's *Guardian,* "the world will be faced with a choice: arable farming either continues to feed the world's animals or it continues to feed the world's people. It cannot do both." Monbiot concludes by describing the vegan diet as "the only ethical response to what is arguably the world's most urgent social justice issue."[3]

All in all, we think the vegan diet is the best ethical response to human hunger, to our current environmental predicament, and to the issue we address in our original mission: respecting the other living, feeling beings with whom we share the planet. Pure vegetarianism is an ethic without borders – between species or between peoples.

George Monbiot's endorsement of the vegan diet allows an exception for holiday gatherings. But, as we hope you'll agree, vegan food tastes wonderful every day, and there is a special joy that comes from serving it at the holidays, surrounded by friends. We look forward to seeing you at the table.

**Using This Cookbook:
Some Practical Considerations**
Preparing pure vegetarian food is an adventure in many ways: an exciting discovery of foods that are healthful for the body and soul, and delicious to

taste. In this book, we share the results of decades – even generations – of culinary adventures. Many of them are perfect for everyday dining; but knowing that vegans have a special interest in sharing their holidays with others, we also provide recipes that have been enjoyed by Priscilla's family at annual holiday gatherings as far back as a family memory goes. Many, we think, taste even better in the pure vegetarian versions developed by Priscilla and the other contributing chefs.

By creating the best foods we can, and asking you to join in the adventure, together we show that good vegan food is not about sacrifice, but about enjoyment and comraderie. With an emphasis on fresh produce and a spectrum of grains, the keynote is variety. Perhaps more so than the typical North American cuisine, we draw on global or influences, from classic Italian pastas to Middle Eastern tabouli; from traditional raw delights such as Mexican guacamole to a soup with roots in West Africa.

Make the most of the recipes in this book by seeking, if you can, fresh seasonal produce at farmers' markets or from your own garden. Some cities give grants to people interested in starting community gardens. Eating with the seasons is a good practice for a number of reasons. It avoids long-distance shipping, and it doesn't expect the

agricultural businesses to harvest produce before its prime, diminishing quality and encouraging the use of artificial enhancements. Equally important is avoiding produce treated with pesticides, which is made easier when we know the origin of the foods we use.

Look for organic fruits and vegetables, as well as other organic ingredients, such as olive oil, pasta, and flour. It's best to avoid ingesting commercial chemicals with your foods, and organic farming leaves less of a footprint on the land which is the other animals' home.

Although vegetarian farming does not intrude on the delicate marine ecosystem, clearly cultivation is required; and voles, rabbits, mice, and pheasants are threatened by planting and harvesting. So there is a special reason here to support vegan organic farmers who are attempting to reduce their impact on the biocommunity. We admire the care they take. Vegan organic farmers adhere to higher standards than the "certified organic" label that is now dispensed by the government.

Organic soybeans that are free from genetic modification are available in most groceries, co-ops, and Asian food shops, in the form of tofu. Soy milk and vegan margarine are also becoming ubiquitous. Soy sour cream and vegan cream cheese is somewhat less common, but a call to your local natural food shop should help you locate it; or check our Ingredients Glossary. You'll find that these ingredients and this book will enable you to create desserts to rival the best chefs' creations.

Finally, a word about health. Many people jump right into a pure vegetarian diet without adverse effects, but if you have a health condition, if you are expecting a new baby, or you are just concerned about eating in a healthful way, it is advisable to consult a professional who is knowledgeable about the vegan diet and lifestyle.[4] John MacDougall, MD and Michael Klaper, MD are two of the most renowned experts in the field, and they offer information in books and electronic sources about vegan nutrition. Many people who change their diets make learning about nutrition one of the benefits of vegetarianism. The core principle for good health is to eat a wide variety of vegetables and fruits, which provide plenty of many vital vitamins and minerals along with a host of other beneficial chemicals.

We believe that everyone, regardless of age, background, or spiritual perspective, can enjoy pure vegetarian food, and will certainly enjoy the recipes to follow. We have carefully chosen a variety of the most attractive, cheerful ideas, designed to be easy on the planet and are respectful of all the earth's inhabitants, whether two-legged, four-legged, winged, finned, or feathered. Priscilla has said, "I have always thought of feeding people as a way of loving them." By sharing these delicious recipes, we hope to fill many lives with love.

Footnotes

1 Alison Leigh Cowan, "The Homeless and the Meatless: A Deer Hunt to Aid the Hungry Brings a Vegan Response," – *The New York Times* at page B1 (10 Dec. 2003).

2 The image was provided by Frances Moore Lappé, author of *Diet For a Small Planet,* based on the high proportion of grains eaten directly in comparatively less affluent regions.

3 George Monbiot, "Why Vegans Were Right All Along" – *The Guardian* (24 Dec. 2002).

4 For general guidance, many vegans have relied on the continuing work of Michael A. Klaper, M.D. Dr. Klaper is a nutritionally-oriented physician, author, and educator. Dr. Klaper has also contributed to the making of two PBS television productions, "Food for Thought," and the award winning "Diet for a New America." On the Internet, see <http://www.drklaper.com/>. Whether or not you use the Internet, telephone consultations are available. Write to Michael A. Klaper, M.D., Professional Health Services, Inc., P.O. Box 1055, Makawao, HI 96768.

Good Morning

Live simply, but enjoy a good breakfast.
The dishes we've selected here will nourish
and support you, and add joy to your day.

Wheat-Free Wild Rice Pancakes

Blueberry Cornmeal Pancakes

French Toast, Free at Last

Scrambled Tofu

Believable "Bacon"

Wheat-Free Wild Rice Pancakes

Makes one generous stack of pancakes

❖ ❖ ❖ ❖ ❖ ❖ ❖ ❖ ❖ ❖ ❖ ❖

½ cup wheat-free Arrowhead Mills Wild Rice Pancake Mix

Ener-G Egg Replacer (mix according to box instructions to make equivalent of 2 eggs)

1 tablespoon canola oil

1 tablespoon brown rice syrup

½ cup vanilla soy milk

¼ teaspoon salt

½ teaspoon ground cinnamon

If you are new to vegan cooking, this might be your introduction to the wondrous powder known as egg replacer. For the vegan chef, a box of egg replacer is a basic, just as flour or cereal is basic to most kitchens. You can find egg replacer at most well-stocked groceries, or at your local health food shop. This is a good way to start out trying it, because these pancakes are a breeze to make, even for late-risers. They are best served hot from the stove, with warmed maple syrup. For added taste and texture, add a fourth-cup of fresh berries or chopped nuts to your batter.

Preparation:
Stir all ingredients just to the point where the lumps disappear. Cook on a heated, lightly oiled griddle or pan, turning when bubbles form on the surface of the pancakes, and the edges begin to dry.

Tip: See the Glossary, under *Shopping Guide,* for information about the ingredients as needed. A few individuals have life-threatening reactions to gluten – a component of many grains, but not rice. As a raw food diet is often gluten-free, people with wheat allergies might find such diets particularly beneficial.

Blueberry Cornmeal Pancakes

Makes twelve 4-inch pancakes

❖ ❖ ❖ ❖ ❖ ❖ ❖ ❖ ❖ ❖ ❖ ❖ ❖

1 cup soy milk

½ cup water

1 cup whole-wheat (or white) pastry flour

½ cup yellow stone-ground cornmeal

1 teaspoon baking powder

½ teaspoon baking soda

¼ teaspoon fine sea salt

1 cup fresh (or thawed frozen) blueberries

Canola or safflower oil

Pure maple syrup, jam, applesauce, or fresh fruit for serving

Here's an unusual idea for cornmeal; you'll never think of pancakes in the same way once you've enjoyed this version. These pancakes are sweetened with berries to help you start your day in a cheery, summertime mood. Thanks to John Robbins, author of *May All Be Fed: Diet For A New World* for this recipe.

Preparation:

Heat the oven to 200 degrees F.

Put the soy milk and water into a small bowl and stir until combined. Whisk the flour, cornmeal, baking powder, baking soda, and salt in a large bowl until combined.

Add the milk mixture and stir to combine, using as few strokes as possible so you do not over-mix the batter. old in the blueberries. Set the batter aside for 5 minutes to thicken.

Lightly oil a frying pan or griddle and heat over medium heat. Using a measuring cup, pour ¼ cupfuls of the pancake batter into the hot pan or onto the hot griddle. Cook until the pancakes are bubbly on top and the edges are slightly dry, 3 to 4 minutes.

Turn and cook for about 3 minutes, until the pancakes are light brown on the bottom. Transfer the pancakes to a baking sheet and keep them warm in the oven while continuing with the remaining batter, oiling the pan between each batch of pancakes.

Serve immediately with maple syrup, jam, applesauce or fresh fruit.

Tip: Please refer to the *Key to Ingredients, Nutrients, and Vegetarian Terms*, in the Glossary at the end of this book, for information about baking powder.

French Toast, Free at Last

Serves 2 to 3
❖ ❖ ❖ ❖ ❖ ❖ ❖ ❖ ❖ ❖ ❖ ❖

2 tablespoons unbleached flour

2 tablespoons nutritional yeast

½ teaspoon salt

1 teaspoon Florida Crystals natural sugar

½ teaspoon cinnamon

¼ teaspoon cardamom

1 cup soy milk

1 tablespoon tahini (sesame butter)

2 tablespoons canola oil

4 to 6 slices of bread

Pure maple syrup for serving

In early 2003, Franco-American political tensions led the chair of the Committee on Administration to rename French toast "freedom toast" in restaurants serving the U.S. House of Representatives. This recipe is the key to a delicious breakfast in the spirit of true freedom: freedom from our reliance on artery-clogging eggs, and freedom for hens to enjoy life on earth in their own way. Bon apétit!

Preparation:
Mix dry ingredients together in bowl, and add soy milk and tahini. Dip bread into batter and fry in oil until brown and crispy on both sides. Serve with pure maple syrup.

Tip: The best thing since sliced bread is, of course, organic sliced bread. Good bets include Ener-G (yeast-free, wheat-free and gluten-free) bread or organic "hearty white" sliced bread from Vermont Bread Co. (Available at health food shops and health-conscious grocers.)

Scrambled Tofu

Serves 3

1 pound extra-firm tofu

2 tablespoons olive oil

1 onion, diced

1 zucchini, thinly sliced

½ red bell pepper, diced

2 cloves of garlic, minced

1 tomato, diced

1 teaspoon dried basil

2 tablespoons tamari

1 teaspoon ground cumin

½ teaspoon turmeric

⅛ teaspoon cayenne pepper

A pinch of freshly ground pepper

½ teaspoon paprika

¼ teaspoon salt

For many of us, a plate of scrambled eggs was the essential breakfast. Could it be that the appeal of scrambled eggs wasn't really the eggs after all, but rather the seasoning and the texture developed by a certain way of cooking them? This recipe will show that you don't have to give up what you liked about the traditional dish, because it's perfectly possible to arrive at the same texture and taste using plant-based ingredients. Next, we have a recipe for Believable "Bacon" from Chef Miyoko Schinner. You might wish to serve these vegan alternatives together.

Preparation:

Drain and crumble the tofu. In a large skillet, heat oil, and add tofu, onion, zucchini, red pepper and garlic. Stir-fry for about 3 minutes.

Add tomato, basil, tamari, cumin, turmeric, paprika, salt, and black and cayenne pepper. Stir-fry until tomatoes are heated through.

Serve immediately, with fresh salsa on the side.

Believable "Bacon"

Serves 2

8 ounces firm tofu, drained

1 tablespoon oil plus nonfat cooking spray, or 2 to 3 tablespoons oil

3 tablespoons nutritional yeast flakes

3 tablespoons soy sauce

1 teaspoon Natural Hickory Liquid Smoke

If you're craving something uncommonly delicious, but uncomplicated to prepare, you've come to the right page. Thanks to Chef Miyoko Schinner, author of *The New Now & Zen Epicure,* here is a creative, aromatic replacement for bacon. Crispy and light, the results provide a delightful addition to a pancake breakfast. And now, mock BLT sandwiches are easy to make.

Preparation:
Cut the tofu into $\frac{1}{8}$-inch-thick slices about the width of a slice of bacon. Heat the oil in a skillet (preferably nonstick), and cook the tofu slices over a medium-low heat until golden brown and crispy on one side. (This can take up to 15 minutes, depending on the pan used.) Flip and cook the other side until browned. The tofu should be very brown and crispy. Sprinkle with the nutritional yeast, then add the soy sauce and liquid smoke, and stir quickly to coat the tofu slices evenly. Cook for another moment, then serve.

Tip: Read about *Liquid Smoke* and *nutritional yeast* in our Glossary under *Key to Ingredients, Nutrients, and Vegetarian Terms.*

Hors D'oeuvre

Share one or two of these tantalizing samplers with guests at your next gathering. They are as pleasing to the eye as they are to the palate and the spirit.

Carrot Pâté

Tapenade and Radishes on Baguette

Toast Cups with Cilantro Pesto

Jumping Bean Dip

Artichoke Spread

Spinach Dip for Raw Vegetables

Végé Boursin

Carrot Pâté

Serves 4

❖ ❖ ❖ ❖ ❖ ❖ ❖ ❖ ❖ ❖ ❖

2 cups carrots, sliced

¼ cup onion, diced

1 clove of garlic, slivered

¼ teaspoon dill

2 tablespoons olive oil

½ cup water

1 tablespoon arrowroot, dissolved in 1 tablespoon water

2 tablespoons white miso

¼ teaspoon salt

2 teaspoons tahini (sesame butter)

Serves four in theory, but there will be a few in every crowd who cannot leave this delightful treat alone for a minute. Many thanks to Chef Ron Pickarski, author of *Friendly Foods,* and to Eco-Cuisine, which copyrighted Chef Ron's original recipe, for making this recipe available to our readers.

Preparation:

In a medium saucepan, sauté the carrots, onions, garlic, and dill in the oil for 2 to 3 minutes. Add the water and cover; simmer about 20 minutes, until the carrots are tender.

Purée the carrot mixture into a smooth paste and return it to the saucepan.

Combine the dissolved arrowroot, miso, salt and tahini. Add this mixture to the puréed carrots. Bring to a slow simmer, stirring constantly, and cook for about 20 minutes until the pâté detaches itself from the side of the pan. Remove from heat.

Turn the pâté mixture out into a lightly oiled serving dish and let cool. Serve the pâté with wheat crisps or as a side dip for vegetables, such as celery.

Tip: We recommend "mellow white miso" listed under *miso* in the *Key to Ingredients, Nutrients, and Vegetarian Terms* in our Glossary.

Tapenade and Radishes on Baguette

Yields 4–6 appetizers

❖ ❖ ❖ ❖ ❖ ❖ ❖ ❖ ❖ ❖ ❖

1 baguette, cut into ½-inch diagonal slices

2 bunches fresh radishes, thinly sliced

¾ cup of pitted Kalamata olives

¼ cup of green, pitted Greek olives

Squeeze of fresh lemon juice

Fresh chives, snipped with scissors into pieces an eighth of an inch long

Sea salt

Fresh ground pepper

This recipe was created by Chef Mark Basile, and it's especially exciting with fresh spring radishes. The olives have enough natural emulsifiers to make additional olive oil optional; if desired, you can add a tablespoon or two for desired consistency. These appetizers may be assembled a few hours ahead of time, and kept in the refrigerator until you are ready to serve them.

Preparation:

Place Kalamata and green olives into a food processor and mix into a rich paste. Add a little squeeze of lemon juice.

Spread the baguette slices (they should be in an oval shape, 2 to 3 inches long) with a thin layer of tapenade. Thinly slice the radishes, and lay the radish rounds over one another, placing them on top of the tapenade in an attractive way. Press lightly to hold in place.

Sprinkle with a little sea salt, fresh ground pepper, and top with a sprinkle of snipped chives. Serve chilled.

Toast Cups with Cilantro Pesto

Makes about 30 to 40 cups

❖ ❖ ❖ ❖ ❖ ❖ ❖ ❖ ❖ ❖ ❖ ❖

1 loaf thinly sliced whole-wheat bread, for toast cups

For cilantro and soy sour cream filling, you'll need:

⅓ cup olive oil

½ cup pine nuts (and extra pine nuts for garnish)

2 cloves garlic

2 large bunches fresh cilantro leaves – washed and dried

Dash of sea salt

Dash of fresh ground pepper

½ cup Tofutti brand Imitation Sour Cream

Fresh lemon juice

Fresh mint leaves

Complemented by fresh mint and cilantro, these miniature pastries will make vegan sour cream a popular and intriguing focal point at your next party. Thanks to Chef Mark Basile for the elegant suggestion.

Preparing the toast cups:
Heat the oven to 350 degrees F.

Cut all crusts off bread, and roll bread slices flat with a rolling pin. Press the bread pieces with your fingers into slightly oiled muffin or tart tins; they will form cupped shapes in the tin container. In small muffin tins, use one slice of rolled bread per muffin cup, and trim excess bread from top of cup.

Bake for nearly 10 minutes, or until toast cups turn golden and begin to crisp. Remove from oven and let cool.

Preparing the pesto filling:
In a food processor, blend cilantro, olive oil, garlic, pine nuts, salt and pepper into a solid paste, adding more oil or nuts if needed, to make pesto consistency. Remove pesto from food processor and place in a bowl. With a wooden spoon, mix pesto with ½ cup soy sour cream. Add salt and pepper to taste. Cover this mixture and chill it.

Assembling the cups:
These are best assembled as near as possible to serving time, but they will hold 1 to 2 hours in the refrigerator without getting too soggy.

Fill cups with pesto mixture. Right before serving, squeeze a small amount of fresh lemon juice over cups. Garnish with a portion of a mint leaf, and 1 to 2 pine nuts.

Tip: Please refer to the Glossary at the end of this book, under *Key to Ingredients, Nutrients, and Vegetarian Terms,* to find out about *Tofutti* vegan products.

Jumping Bean Dip

Makes 2½ cups

❖ ❖ ❖ ❖ ❖ ❖ ❖ ❖ ❖ ❖

10 sun-dried tomatoes

2 roasted red peppers (from a jar)

1 fresh, seeded, and chopped jalapeño pepper

1 teaspoon minced garlic

One 15.5-ounce can of Northern beans, drained; or the equivalent in dried Northern beans, soaked and cooked

7 ounces soft tofu

1 teaspoon dried cumin

1 teaspoon dried oregano

¼ cup olive oil

½ teaspoon salt

Ground pepper

Nothing like jalapeño peppers to build character. And here's a dip that has the courage of its convictions. Serve it with raw vegetables, or as a spicy cracker spread.

Preparation:
In food processor, purée sun-dried tomatoes, roasted peppers, jalapeño pepper and garlic. Add beans and blend. Next add the soft tofu, cumin, oregano, salt, and pepper to taste. While blending, drizzle with olive oil.

Artichoke Spread

Makes about 2 cups

❖ ❖ ❖ ❖ ❖ ❖ ❖ ❖ ❖ ❖ ❖

14-ounce can artichoke hearts (packed in water)

1 clove peeled and mashed garlic

3 tablespoons Nayonaise or Vegenaise

Paprika

You might wish to keep these ingredients handy. This spread gives your guests a warm welcome; yet it can be whipped up at the last minute if company shows up unexpectedly.

Preparation:
Drain artichokes. Chop artichokes finely and transfer to small saucepan. Add garlic and Nayonaise, and blend. Warm over low heat, stirring constantly. Do not let the mixture boil. Turn spread into a serving bowl. Sprinkle with paprika and serve with crackers.

Tip: Please refer to the Glossary at the end of this book, under *Key to Ingredients, Nutrients, and Vegetarian Terms,* to find out about *Nayonaise.*

Spinach Dip for Raw Vegetables

Makes about 2 cups

❖ ❖ ❖ ❖ ❖ ❖ ❖ ❖ ❖ ❖ ❖

1 package frozen chopped spinach, thawed

½ cup chopped parsley or dill

½ cup chopped scallions (mainly the white parts)

1 cup Tofutti brand Imitation Sour Cream

¾ cup Nayonaise or Vegenaise

½ teaspoon salt

½ teaspoon pepper

This blend makes a vibrant green crudité dip; but start early. For best results, you'll need to let this set dip overnight in the refrigerator.

Preparation:
Squeeze the spinach dry. Blend it and all other ingredients in a blender until smooth. Refrigerate the dip overnight before enjoying it.

Tip: Are you another admirer of dill? You can dry dill weed, but it is actually better to chop up what you need, and keep the rest in the freezer. Please refer to the Glossary at the end of this book, under *Key to Ingredients, Nutrients, and Vegetarian Terms,* to find out about *Nayonaise* and *Tofutti* vegan products.

Végé Boursin

Makes 3½ cups

❖ ❖ ❖ ❖ ❖ ❖ ❖ ❖ ❖ ❖ ❖

½ cup vegan margarine, at room temperature

Two 8-ounce packages of (Tofutti brand) Imitation Cream Cheese

2 cloves garlic, pressed

½ teaspoon dried oregano

¼ teaspoon dried basil

¼ teaspoon dried thyme

¼ teaspoon dried marjoram

¼ teaspoon dried dill weed

¼ teaspoon ground pepper

Boursin cheese has become popular in the gourmet sections of North American groceries, but as we shall see, it is actually the unique combination of herbs that impart its special taste. This sumptuous Boursin pâté will impress connoisseurs, and if cows could talk, they would probably say "C'est une bonne idée!"

Preparation:
Blend the cream cheese and margarine by hand until smooth. Add seasonings and mix well. Chill overnight, and serve, slightly chilled, with crackers.

Tip: Please refer to the Glossary at the end of this book, under *Key to Ingredients, Nutrients, and Vegetarian Terms,* to find out about vegan *margarine* and *Tofutti* vegan products.

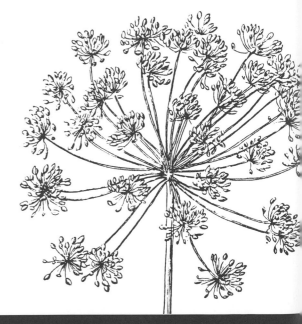

Soups

Let the essence of good soup warm your soul.
We blend the collective wisdom from a variety of
cultures here, in this generous array of soups for
all seasons.

Perfect Chestnut Soup

Zucchini Soup

Mark's Black Bean Soup

Cream of Broccoli Soup

Macaroni and Bean Soup
(Pasta e Fagioli)

Cream of Cauliflower Soup with Chives

Vegetable Bisque

Creamy Lima Bean Soup

West African Peanut Soup

Yellow Split Pea Soup

Asparagus Soup

Lentil Soup

Greek Bean Soup

Carrot and Potato Soup

Veggiessoise

Perfect Chestnut Soup

Serves 6

8 tablespoons vegan margarine

4 cups whole roasted chestnuts (about 1½ pounds)

1 carrot, peeled and chopped

1 leek, mostly white parts, well rinsed and chopped

1 parsnip, peeled and chopped

1 cup celery, chopped

7½ cups vegetable broth

½ cup Madeira wine

2 or more parsley sprigs, chopped

Pinch of grated nutmeg

Sea salt

Fresh ground pepper

Tofutti brand Imitation Sour Cream

Cayenne pepper

Chestnuts are surprisingly low in fat. They're also highly perishable, so store them in a plastic bag in your refrigerator until you're ready to cook. This recipe was adapted from a recipe from Delmarvelous Chestnuts, a chestnut grower in Townsend, Delaware. We're pleased to offer our friends a vegan version of the experts' festive winter soup.

Preparation:

To roast chestnuts: Choose fresh, firm, unwrinkled chestnuts with no signs of spores. On the flat side of each chestnut, take a small knife and cut an "X" from one end to the other. Make sure you cut all the way through the shell. Lay the chestnuts in one layer in an oven-proof dish. Bake at 325 degrees F for about 25–30 minutes, until the cuts peel back naturally from the heat. Cool only slightly. Peel off the outer shell and the fuzzy skin, and set nuts aside.

In a heavy saucepan, melt 4 tablespoons of the margarine over medium heat. Add chestnuts and sauté until heated through, about 5 minutes. Set aside.

Melt the remaining 4 tablespoons of margarine in heavy, large soup pot over medium heat. Add carrot, parsnip, leek and celery; sauté until soft, about 7 minutes. Add vegetable broth and bring to boil. Reduce heat to low. Add the chestnuts, Madeira wine, parsley, nutmeg, salt and pepper. Continue to simmer for another 15 minutes.

Purée the soup in batches in a food processor or blender. Transfer the puréed soup to a large soup pot and reheat, stirring frequently.

When it's thoroughly heated, ladle the soup into bowls. Top it off with a dollop of non-dairy sour cream and sprinkle slightly with cayenne pepper.

Tip: Please refer to the Glossary at the end of this book, under *Key to Ingredients, Nutrients, and Vegetarian Terms,* to find out about *Tofutti* vegan products, including sour cream.

Zucchini Soup

Serves 6 to 8 people

Vegetable broth:

3 medium zucchini, coarsely chopped

4 large carrots, coarsely chopped

2 medium onions, coarsely chopped

6 unpeeled potatoes, coarsely chopped

Several tablespoons olive oil for sautéing

2 cups parsley, chopped

1 teaspoon salt

Soup ingredients:

1 clove of garlic, chopped

2 medium zucchini, diced

1½ cups fresh basil, coarsely chopped

1½ cups fresh tarragon, coarsely chopped

2 pinches cayenne pepper

3 tablespoons olive oil

Sea salt

Fresh ground pepper

Light yet satisfying, this soup combines just the right herbs and spices. In Québec, zucchini, which belong to the gourd family, are known as courgettes.

Preparation for vegetable broth:
Sauté 3 zucchini, carrots, onions and potatoes in several tablespoons of olive oil. As vegetables lightly brown, stir in parsley, salt, and enough water to cover vegetables. Simmer, covered, for 30 minutes. Remove from heat, drain and discard vegetables. Set broth aside to be added to soup.

Preparation for soup:
In large soup pot, sauté 1 chopped clove of garlic in 3 tablespoons olive oil until golden. Add 2 diced zucchini and stir to coat with oil. Add 1 to 1½ cups chopped basil, and 1 to 1½ cups chopped tarragon. Add 2 pinches of cayenne pepper, and salt and pepper to taste. Stir briefly, then add the vegetable broth into the soup.

After broth and soup are merged:
Simmer, partially covered, for 20 minutes until zucchini is barely soft.

Purée ⅔ of the full mixture in a food processor, return this to a pot, re-heat, and stir with remaining mixture. Serve hot.

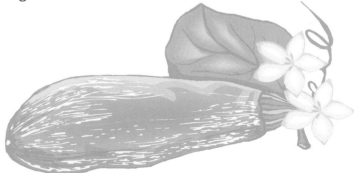

Mark's Black Bean Soup

Serves 4 to 6

2 tablespoons extra virgin olive oil

1½ cups diced carrots

1½ cups diced onions

1 cup diced celery

1 tablespoon minced garlic

½ teaspoon sea salt

½ teaspoon ground pepper

8 cups vegetable broth

¼ cup marinara sauce (tomato sauce)

1 tablespoon tamari

4 cups cooked black beans (soaked overnight before cooking)

½ cup chopped parsley

½ cup scallions

This hearty winter soup comes to our table thanks to Chef Mark Shadle, author of the cookbook *It's Only Natural.* With its delightful range of herbs, this soup tastes even better the following day, after marinating. If you prefer to serve this soup on the day you make it, let it sit at least an hour, and then reheat the amount needed.

Preparation:
Heat large soup pot briefly, then add oil. Sauté the diced carrots, onions, and celery and the minced garlic. Then add the oregano, basil, broth, marinara sauce, tamari and beans. Simmer for 30 minutes and then add the parsley and scallions, and additional salt and pepper if desired.

Tip: You'll find marinara sauce described in the Glossary.

Cream of Broccoli Soup

Serves 6

1 cup raw cashews

5 cups vegetable stock or vegetable bouillon

2 medium boiling potatoes, unpeeled, cut into ½-inch cubes

1 medium onion, finely chopped

1 bunch broccoli, trimmed and coarsely chopped

1 teaspoon dried basil

1 teaspoon fine sea salt

¼ teaspoon freshly ground pepper

Here's a soup that has to be great to be good. Priscilla searched far and wide for this greatness, to finally find it in *May All Be Fed: Diet For A New World* – thanks to our friend John Robbins. It is lightly cooked and promptly served, so as to retain the broccoli's lively hue.

Preparation:
Blend the cashews with a cup of the vegetable stock in a blender for about a minute, until you have a smooth consistency. Place the remaining 4 cups vegetable stock with the potatoes and onion in a large pot. Bring to a simmer, cover, and cook for 5 minutes. Stir in the broccoli and basil and return to a simmer. Cover and cook for about 10 minutes until the potatoes are tender. Stir in the reserved cashew mixture, the salt, and pepper and bring just to a simmer.

Let the mixture cool slightly. Transfer about half of the soup to a blender and lightly purée. Return the purée to the pot and stir well. Serve immediately.

Macaroni and Bean Soup *(Pasta e Fagioli)*

Serves 4 to 6

❖ ❖ ❖ ❖ ❖ ❖ ❖ ❖ ❖ ❖

1½ cups small pasta shells (the size of Ronzoni's #23 shells)

2 tablespoons olive oil

1 large, finely chopped onion

½ finely chopped clove of garlic

1 cup finely chopped celery

2 cups marinara sauce

½ teaspoon salt

1 tablespoon chopped parsley

⅛ teaspoon pepper

1 quart warm water

2 cups cooked white beans (or 1 can with liquid)

One tablespoon grated soy Parmesan cheese (optional)

The peasants of northern Italy would harvest beans and spread the bean pods over the pavement in the yards to absorb the autumn sun, and then store them. During the frigid winter, fagioli pots would bubble with beans. Hence the inspiration for this hearty soup, which came to the Americas along with Italian immigrants. The soup can be prepared a couple of days ahead, for – delicious as it is when first prepared – it gets even better as it marinates.

Preparation:
Heat olive oil in large saucepan. Add onions, celery, garlic and brown lightly. Stir in marinara sauce, parsley, salt and pepper; cook for 10 minutes. Add warm water and beans, and bring to a boil. Cook for about 10 more minutes. Stir in pasta shells and boil uncovered for 15 minutes, or until tender. Stir frequently to prevent pasta from sticking. Serve piping hot.

Add grated soy Parmesan cheese if desired. To reheat, stir in boiling water to desired consistency, and heat over low flame.

Tip: Please refer to *Key to Ingredients, Nutrients, and Vegetarian Terms,* in the Glossary at the end of this book (under *cheese*), to find out about soy (vegan) Parmesan cheese. Marinara sauce is also described in the Glossary.

Cream of Cauliflower Soup with Chives

Serves 10

❖ ❖ ❖ ❖ ❖ ❖ ❖ ❖ ❖ ❖ ❖ ❖ ❖

4 leeks, mostly white parts, well rinsed and chopped

½ cup celery root, diced

½ cup fennel, diced

2 to 3 tablespoons soy margarine

1 head cauliflower, broken into large florets

6 cups vegetable broth

1 teaspoon salt

¼ teaspoon pepper

1 tablespoon fresh thyme leaves

1 cup soy milk creamer

2 tablespoons chopped fresh chives

Cream of Cauliflower is known to many chefs as Crème DuBarry, after a noble of Louis IV's day. Celery root and fennel add an unusual zing to this version of a traditionally understated recipe.

Preparation:

Cook the leeks, celery root, and fennel in the margarine over medium-low heat in an uncovered large pot for about 10 minutes, until the vegetables become tender. Add the cauliflower and cook for 10 additional minutes. Add the vegetable broth, salt, pepper and thyme, and bring to a boil over high heat. Reduce heat to low and simmer for about 30 to 40 minutes, until vegetables are very soft. In a food processor, purée the soup until smooth. Return the purée to the pot, add the non-dairy creamer, and warm on medium until heated throughout. Adjust seasoning to taste, and sprinkle chives over the top.

Vegetable Bisque

Serves 6 to 8

❖ ❖ ❖ ❖ ❖ ❖ ❖ ❖ ❖ ❖ ❖ ❖

¾ cup (or 1½ sticks) vegan margarine

¾ cup diced onion

1½ cups diced potatoes

¾ cup peeled diced tomato

¾ cup diced carrot

¾ cup diced green beans

¾ cup coarsely chopped broccoli

¾ cup leeks, mostly white parts, well rinsed and minced

¾ cup minced zucchini

1 garlic clove minced

1½ teaspoons Florida Crystals natural sugar, or enough to give desired taste

Sea salt

Fresh ground pepper

1½ quarts (6 cups) vegetable broth

½ cup soy milk or coconut milk creamer

Chopped parsley for garnish

This velvety soup is especially welcome when the weather outside is nippy. A garnish of fresh parsley adds a fresh taste and a bit of contrast. Serve with salad and crusty bread.

Preparation:
Melt margarine in large stockpot over medium-high heat. Add onion and sauté for 1 to 2 minutes. Reduce heat to low and add remaining ingredients except broth, soy creamer and parsley. Cook for about 20 to 25 minutes, until vegetables are soft but not browned.

Add broth and bring to boil over medium-high heat. Reduce heat and simmer about 10 minutes. Let the mixture cool slightly.

Transfer the mixture to a blender or processor in batches, and purée until smooth, leaving some texture in the soup. Taste the soup and adjust seasoning. Return the soup to the stockpot, place it over medium heat, and gradually stir in the soy creamer. Heat the soup but do not boil it. Garnish each serving with chopped parsley.

Tip: Please refer to the *Key to Ingredients, Nutrients, and Vegetarian Terms,* in the Glossary at the end of this book (under *Florida Crystals* natural sugar and vegan *margarine*), for some words to the wise about both.

Creamy Lima Bean Soup

Serves 6

❖ ❖ ❖ ❖ ❖ ❖ ❖ ❖ ❖ ❖ ❖

1½ cups dry lima beans, thoroughly washed

6 cups vegetable broth

Sesame oil

2 cups finely diced onions

1 cup peeled and coarsely grated carrots

2 tablespoons chopped garlic

2 tablespoons olive oil

¼ teaspoon ground pepper

½ cup finely diced green bell pepper

1 tablespoon sea salt or less

¼ teaspoon ground coriander

Finely shredded scallions (including tops) for garnish

Inventive lima bean soups were an important part of Native American culture. If it's been a while since you've had lima beans, let them make a comeback. You'll be pleasantly surprised by the results of this recipe, adapted from Chef Ron Pickarski's cookbook *Friendly Foods.*

Preparation:

To prepare the beans, bring the vegetable broth to a simmer in a large saucepan and add the beans. Immediately remove from heat, let the mixture cool, and refrigerate for several hours or overnight. Cook the beans in the soaking broth covered over medium heat about 1½ hours, until tender.

To make the soup, sauté the onions, carrots, and garlic in a 2-quart saucepan with the olive oil and pepper over medium heat until the onions are translucent. Add a few drops of sesame oil.

In a blender, purée 2 cups of cooked lima beans with 2 cups of the soup's broth. Add this purée to the sautéed vegetables. Add the remaining cup of cooked lima beans, keeping them whole. Then add the bell peppers, salt and coriander to the bean mixture and cook for a few minutes to blend the spices.

Serve with a garnish of finely shredded scallions.

West African Peanut Soup

Serves 4 to 6

❖ ❖ ❖ ❖ ❖ ❖ ❖ ❖ ❖ ❖ ❖ ❖

1 tablespoon peanut or canola oil

2 cups chopped onion

2 stalks of celery, diced

1 cup sliced carrot

2 cups cubed sweet potatoes (peeled)

1 teaspoon grated fresh ginger

½ teaspoon cayenne (less if you prefer a milder taste)

4 cups vegetable stock (or water)

2 cups tomato juice

1 cup smooth peanut butter

1 cup chopped scallions (mainly white parts)

Called "groundnut stew" in Africa, this dish has found popularity throughout North America. Groundnuts, or peanuts, are originally South American, and were grown by indigenous South American farmers. They were introduced to West Africa by the Portuguese in the 16th century.

Enslaved Africans popularized peanuts in North America and they also introduced peanut soup to colonial North America. Peanut soup is still served at George Washington's Mount Vernon home and Colonial Williamsburg, Virginia. Africans also gave the peanut one of its many nicknames: The (West African) Kikongo word for peanut is nguba, or, as they say in the southeastern United States, goober.[5]

Preparation:

Sauté the onion and celery in oil, stirring in the cayenne pepper and ginger. Add the carrots, sweet potato and vegetable broth, and bring to boil. Cover, reduce heat, and cook until the vegetables are tender.

Allow the soup to cool somewhat, and then purée it in batches; return all to the pot. Stir in the tomato juice and peanut butter; heat until all ingredients are thoroughly mixed and hot; stir in scallions and serve.

5 See "A Taste of Ghana" Glossary, available electronically at http://www.ghana.co.uk/food/Glossary/Others.htm (citing *The Congo Cookbook*).

Yellow Split Pea Soup

Serves 4

2 to 3 tablespoons olive oil

1 onion, diced

3 stalks of celery, diced

3 carrots, diced

1 cup washed, dried yellow split peas

1 potato, chopped in bite-sized chunks

6 cups vegetable broth

1 teaspoon curry powder

1 bay leaf

½ teaspoon thyme

Sea salt

Ground pepper

Made with yellow split peas, which are milder than split green peas, this soup has a gentle base. Slightly curried, this version picks up a hint of South Asian style.

Preparation:
Sauté onion, celery and carrots in olive oil for several minutes in soup pot. Add the dry split peas, vegetable broth, curry powder, bay leaf, thyme, potato, salt, and pepper. Simmer over medium-low heat for 1 hour, or longer until the peas are soft.

Asparagus Soup

Serves 4

❖ ❖ ❖ ❖ ❖ ❖ ❖ ❖ ❖ ❖ ❖

2 tablespoons canola oil

2½ cups chopped asparagus stalks and tips

1½ cups leeks, mostly white parts, well rinsed and chopped

¼ cup chopped celery

1 teaspoon minced fresh garlic

1 bay leaf

6 cups vegetable broth

½ cup soy milk creamer

1 teaspoon salt

Ground pepper

Asparagus is a traditional spring vegetable. Leeks and celery complement it gently. To enjoy this soup at its best, serve it at a springtime gathering.

Preparation:
Prepare the asparagus by discarding the tough ends.

Heat the oil in a 4-quart pot, and add the asparagus, leeks, celery, garlic, bay leaf. Sauté over medium-low heat, stirring frequently, for 10 minutes. Add the vegetable broth; simmer, partially covered, for about 20 minutes over medium-low heat.

Let cool slightly; then purée mixture in a blender in batches. Return the purée to the pot, season with salt, and pepper to taste. Add soy creamer, and heat thoroughly.

Tip: Please refer to the *Key to Ingredients, Nutrients, and Vegetarian Terms,* in the Glossary at the end of this book (under *vegan margarine*), for some words to the wise about vegan margarine.

Lentil Soup

Serves 4

❖ ❖ ❖ ❖ ❖ ❖ ❖ ❖ ❖ ❖ ❖

1½ cups washed lentils

6 cups salted cold water

2 large, chopped carrots

1 medium, chopped onion

2 stalks celery, chopped

2 tablespoons olive oil

1½ or 2 cups canned tomatoes

Sea salt

Ground pepper

Lentils have a long and varied history; they've been a food source for over 8,000 years. The boiled lentils in this recipe provide calcium, phosphorus, magnesium, folacin, iron, and potassium. And of the dried vegetables, the lentil is second only to the soybean in protein content. But this Lentil Soup is second to none. Enjoy it with crusty bread, or as the start to any good Mediterranean-style meal.

Preparation:
Cook lentils in water for 45 minutes in a pan partially covered with a lid. Add vegetables, oil, tomatoes and salt and pepper to taste. Simmer for 30 minutes. Stir often.

Greek Bean Soup

Serves 4

❖ ❖ ❖ ❖ ❖ ❖ ❖ ❖ ❖ ❖ ❖ ❖

1 can cannellini beans, or 1 cup dried beans, soaked in water overnight and cooked until tender

1½ carrots, chopped

2 celery stalks, with leaves

1 medium onion, chopped

14-ounce can Italian plum tomatoes

¼ cup olive oil

2 cups vegetable broth

Fresh Italian parsley, chopped

Sea salt

Ground pepper

Served with your choice of bread and a mixed green salad, this soup is likely to become one of your life's simple pleasures. Cannellini are white kidney beans, very popular with vegetables in Greece. Thus, during the 1890s, a taste for these beans was imported along with Greek migration to New York, Chicago, and the textile town of Lowell, Massachusetts, and soon to Detroit, Boston and St. Louis.

Preparation:
Dice the following by hand: 1½ carrots, 2 stalks celery and their leaves, 1 medium onion.

Heat ¼ cup olive oil in soup kettle and sauté carrots. After 5 minutes, add onions, then celery. When all vegetables are light medium brown, add 1 teaspoon salt, pepper and canned tomatoes. Simmer, covered, for 10 minutes. Add 2 cups of vegetable broth and cook for another 10 minutes, or until vegetables are tender. Add the cooked cannellini beans. Add more broth if needed and decorate with a fresh sprinkling of chopped parsley.

Carrot and Potato Soup

Generously serves 4

❖ ❖ ❖ ❖ ❖ ❖ ❖ ❖ ❖ ❖ ❖ ❖

A dash of cold-pressed olive oil

3 to 5 carrots, chopped

1 onion, sliced

3 to 5 potatoes, cubed

1 clove garlic, minced

6 cups vegetable stock

¼ teaspoon powdered ginger

2 teaspoons curry powder

A few dashes of tamari

Sea salt

Ground pepper

This soup brings a hint of ginger and spice to the popular combination of carrots and potatoes. As always, we recommend using organic olive oil.

Preparation:
In a soup pot, sauté the onions and garlic in oil. Add the vegetable stock, carrots, and potatoes, and bring to a boil. Lower to simmer and add curry, ginger, and salt and pepper to taste. Cook the mixture until the potatoes are tender. Take out half of the solids, and purée in a food processor or blender. Return the purée to the pot. Heat thoroughly.

Veggiessoise

Serves about 8

❖ ❖ ❖ ❖ ❖ ❖ ❖ ❖ ❖ ❖ ❖ ❖ ❖

3 tablespoons vegan margarine

8 large leeks, mostly white parts, well rinsed and chopped

3 medium russet potatoes, peeled and thinly sliced

5 cups vegetable broth

1 cup soy milk creamer

Pinch of sea salt

¼ teaspoon freshly cracked black pepper, or to taste

2 or more tablespoons fresh, chopped chives

Vichyssoise was introduced in New York City, in or about 1917, at the Ritz-Carlton Hotel. Chef Louis Diat called the potato and leek soup Crème Vichyssoise Glacée, or Chilled Cream Vichyssoise, after Vichy, "the famous spa located not 20 miles from our Bourbonnaise home, as a tribute to the fine cooking of the region." Diat remembered how his mother, Annette Alajoinine Diat, would cool his breakfast soup on a warm morning by adding cold milk to it. An extra straining, and a sprinkle of chives, et voilà: Chef Diat named the new version of his mother's soup."[6]

During World War II, some chefs tried to change the name to "Crème Gauloise Glacée" when a government collaborating with the Nazis was set up in the French town of Vichy.

Obviously, the change didn't stick. But we take the liberty of changing its name once again here, with due respect to the Diat family, as we replace the usual chicken stock and dairy cream found in the soup with more peaceful ingredients.

Preparation:
Melt the margarine in a large soup pot, over low heat.

Add the leeks and cook for about 20 minutes, stirring, until tender but not browned. Add the potatoes and vegetable broth, and bring to boil. Reduce heat and simmer, partially covered, for about 30 minutes until the potatoes are soft. Purée until smooth. Stir in 1 cup soy creamer. Thin, if necessary, with additional vegetable broth. Season with salt and black pepper to taste.

Refrigerate and serve cold, garnishing each cup with snipped, fresh chives.

Tip: Veggiessoise should be pronounced, following its original, as "veggie-swahz" as the "e" after the final "s" means the latter is pronounced rather than silent.

6 Louis Diat, *Cooking à la Ritz* (1941).

Raw Delights

Raw food chefs often call them "living foods" – dishes which are naturally rich in enzymes because they have not been heated over 118 degrees F (although some raw chefs will use dehydrators at slightly higher settings; maximum allowable temperatures are, so to speak, hotly debated). Enzymes are essential for good digestion and vitality, and many enzymes are retained in dehydrated or frozen foods. Processed foods, however, have had the enzymes pasteurized or cooked out of them. The living food diet has become increasingly popular, with the advent of such restaurants as the intimate and arty Quintessence in Manhattan.

A raw food vegan diet may be defined in various ways, but usually at least four-fifths of its weight is made up of fresh, uncooked plants. Leafy greens and broccoli, rich in zinc, calcium, and protein, form a key part of raw diets. Such vegetables also provide vitamin K, which promotes healthy bones. Additionally, raw carrots provide calcium, and peas provide zinc and protein. For beneficial fats, the raw diet frequently includes olives, avocados, almonds, hazelnuts and macadamias. It is also important to include a good source of omega-3 fats such as flax seed oil.

To some extent, humans may have evolved to rely on cooking. This is why the Vegan Society recommends a varied diet including both cooked and raw foods as the proven basis for vegan health, particularly for infants and children who need a relatively high calorie density. Although cooking destroys some nutrients, conservative cooking – such as steaming or boiling – causes only modest loss of some nutrients. Cooking increases the energy available from starches in potatoes and grains, and inactivates certain food toxins, thereby increasing the range of foods available to us. Is our broader range an optimal diet? Today, the question remains open.

We do know that raw food has environmental advantages: It requires little packaging and no gas, oil, or electricity to prepare. It also inspires creativity. Many North American cities and towns now have groups, made of people from all walks of life, who meet and share raw recipes. Here is a sampling of raw delights, from the traditional to the unusual, to whet your appetite.

"The day is coming when a single carrot, freshly observed, will set off a revolution." PAUL CÉZANNE

Creamy Cucumber Gazpacho

Serves 6

❖ ❖ ❖ ❖ ❖ ❖ ❖ ❖ ❖ ❖

4 cups cold tomato and vegetable juice (such as R.W. Knudsen's "Very Veggie")

1 small, finely minced onion

2 to 3 large, freshly diced tomatoes

1 cup minced green pepper

1 diced cucumber

1 clove crushed garlic

2 scallions (both green and white parts), chopped

2 celery stalks, diced

Juice of ½ fresh lemon

Juice of 1 fresh lime

2 tablespoons wine vinegar

1 teaspoon tarragon

1 teaspoon basil

¼ cup fresh, chopped parsley

Dash of ground cumin

Dash of hot sauce (optional)

2 tablespoons olive oil

Sea salt

Fresh ground pepper

One teaspoon agave nectar (optional)

Gazpacho's enduring popularity throughout the Americas has resulted in a great many variations. However made, it's best with ripe, locally grown tomatoes. Our version, Creamy Cucumber Gazpacho, is sure to give you or your guests a lift on a hot day.

Preparation:

Chop the ingredients finely in food processor, including salt and pepper to taste. Chill combined ingredients for at least two hours in a pitcher. Chilling overnight is the best bet for a thorough blending of your ingredients. Bring the pitcher of gazpacho out of the refrigerator for 1 hour before serving, so that it is cool, but not cold enough to dull the lively combination of tastes.

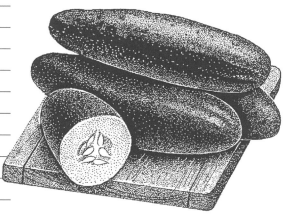

Guacamole

Serves 4

❖ ❖ ❖ ❖ ❖ ❖ ❖ ❖ ❖ ❖ ❖

2 avocados, peeled and seeded

1 scallion (mainly whites), finely chopped

½ small red onion, diced

2 cloves minced garlic

1 jalapeño pepper, seeded and minced

1 fresh lime, juiced

½ tomato, diced

2 tablespoons chopped fresh cilantro

Sea salt

Serve guacamole with tortilla chips or raw flax crisps. For a completely raw snack that is easy to prepare, offer it as an accompaniment to cut vegetables such as jícama and carrot sticks.

Preparation:

Choose an avocado that has give to it. Peel and seed the avocado and mash it with a fork. Transfer the mashed avocado to a bowl and combine with remaining ingredients, including salt to taste. Cover and refrigerate for up to 2 hours.

Tip: A pit left in the guacamole, and a sprinkling of lemon or lime juice, helps to preserve the guacamole's hue of vibrant green. Stir lightly before serving.

Spicy Hijiki *(Hiziki)* Salad

Serves 6

❖ ❖ ❖ ❖ ❖ ❖ ❖ ❖ ❖ ❖

Salad:

1 cup loosely packed, dried hijiki seaweed

3 cups cut broccoli (mostly florets, cut in half, with small, peeled, sliced stems)

3 cups coarsely cut or sliced green cabbage

2 cups thinly sliced fresh shitaki mushrooms

1 small red bell pepper, finely diced

Marinade:

Three separate batches, with each batch containing:

2 tablespoons tamari (Nama Shoyu)

1 tablespoon Asian sesame oil

2 tablespoons juice of a fresh lemon

½ teaspoon minced garlic

½ teaspoon minced fresh ginger

Light sprinkle of Spanish paprika

5 tablespoons water

This recipe requires 2 hours time for marinating, but is easy to prepare and well worth the wait. Our thanks go to Susan Lerner, photographer and raw foodist. We spotted Susan's stunning salad at a raw vegan potluck hosted in November 2003 in Bethesda, Maryland by Steve Seuser, member of the Vegetarian Society of D.C.

Soak hijiki in fresh water for two hours; it will almost quadruple in size.

While hijiki is soaking, begin to marinate vegetables. Marinate the broccoli and cabbage in two separate batches first for an hour, to fully tenderize them. Marinate mushrooms in third marinade batch (½ hour); drain hijiki of water and add to mushroom marinade. Mix together three batches; marinate for half an hour.

Add diced red pepper, and serve.

Classic Mediterranean Salad with Fresh Mint

Serves 6 to 8

❖ ❖ ❖ ❖ ❖ ❖ ❖ ❖ ❖ ❖ ❖

Salad:

1 head of romaine lettuce, torn

3 tomatoes, diced

1 sliced cucumber

1 small green bell pepper, sliced and seeds removed

1 small onion, cut into rings

6 radishes, thinly sliced

1 cup chopped parsley

Dressing:

6 tablespoons olive oil

Juice of 2 fresh lemons

A pinch of pepper

2/3 teaspoon salt

1 pressed or finely minced garlic clove

A handful of mint leaves, minced

Make a perfect restaurant-style salad at home with this recipe. If they're available, organic easter egg radishes are especially decorative. Always dress green salads at the very last minute, starting with a hint of dressing and adding more if needed – or inviting your guests to do so. You might also wish to top this one off with a dollop of Tabouli (recipe follows) or, if your event is not all-raw, serve it with any of our *Classic Pasta Dishes*.

Preparation:

Discard the wet seeds from the cut tomatoes and add the diced parts to the lettuce. Toss with cucumber, pepper, onion, radishes, and parsley in a bowl.

Whisk together olive oil, lemon and pepper, and the salt, garlic and mint as a dressing to serve on the side.

Tabouli

Serves 4
❖ ❖ ❖ ❖ ❖ ❖ ❖ ❖ ❖ ❖ ❖

1 cup bulgur wheat

1 cup water

3 tablespoons olive oil

Juice of 1 lemon

½ cup fresh parsley, minced

1 generous tablespoon minced mint leaves

1 generous tablespoon sweet red pepper, thinly sliced then chopped

6 to 8 Kalamata olives, removed from the pit and coarsely chopped

1 teaspoon grated lemon zest

½ teaspoon salt

This popular Middle Eastern salad makes a quick and refreshing summer dish. It's nicely paired with the *Classic Mediterranean Salad with Fresh Mint* (preceding recipe) and warmed pita bread. If your gathering is not all-raw, you may wish to serve this with *Baba Ghanouj,* under *Sandwiches and Spreads.*

Preparation:
Make tabouli by mixing the dry bulgur wheat with the water, olive oil, and lemon juice; set aside to marinate for 1 hour. Stir in the parsley, mint, lemon zest, chopped red pepper and olives, and salt.

Tips: Tabouli (see Glossary under *Key to Ingredients, Nutrients, and Vegetarian Terms;* it is also written as "tabbouleh" and "tabbuli") can be made from simple bulgur wheat from the bulk foods section of health food shops, co-ops, or grocers with good bulk food sections.

Fiery Salsa

Serves 3

❖ ❖ ❖ ❖ ❖ ❖ ❖ ❖ ❖ ❖ ❖

1 tablespoon of fresh lime juice

1 clove garlic, minced

6 scallions (mainly the white parts), chopped

1 or 2 jalapeño peppers, minced

1 tablespoon fresh cilantro, chopped

1 cup ripe tomatoes, diced

½ teaspoon salt

¼ teaspoon freshly ground pepper

2 tablespoons red onion, chopped

¼ teaspoon ground cumin

¼ cup tomato or vegetable juice

Salsa and tortilla chips are always popular with guests, or as a surprise for groups at meetings and other events.

Preparation:
Combine all ingredients and serve at room temperature.

Tip: If you use fresh jalapeños, it is a good idea to remove the seeds. This dish is the perfect complement to Scrambled Tofu (see the *Good Morning* section).

Gardener's Delight Fettuccini

Serves 4 to 6

❖ ❖ ❖ ❖ ❖ ❖ ❖ ❖ ❖ ❖

5 large zucchini

1 cup tahini (sesame butter)

¾ cup fresh parsley, finely chopped

1 tablespoon garlic powder

1 large onion, chopped

2 teaspoons black pepper

1 cup fresh lemon juice

One tablespoon sea salt (optional)

½ cup pine nuts, very finely ground

2 tablespoons oregano

1 tablespoon thyme

1 cup mushrooms, chopped

½ cup olive oil

1 cup water

½ cup chopped scallions

Here's a true indigenous recipe, which can be made from zucchini or other available squash. "Squash" is short for the word "askutasquash" from the Narragansett language and meaning "eaten raw." Other Native American tribes had similar words: The Iroquois called it "isquoutersquash."

The raw dish we feature here was perhaps most notably popularized in more modern days by the Zucchini Fettuccine created by Imar Hutchins, author of *30 Days at Delights of the Garden.* The dish of noodles is made from the chef's preferred squash. Make thin noodles from the squash using a mandoline vegetable slicer. Prepare an oil and vinegar dressing, such as *Fresh Herb Vinaigrette* in our *Traditional Salads and Dressings* section. Or experiment with your own mix of Dijon mustard, dill, shallot and pure maple syrup. Here is Imar's original version.

Preparation:
Make thin noodles from the squash using a mandoline vegetable slicer; then soak them with water, onions, mushrooms, and oil in separate bowl. In a food processor, blend tahini, lemon juice, parsley, and spices. Then blend in pine nuts and scallions. Add this mixture to the zucchini and mushrooms that are soaking; mix well. This dish takes about 30 minutes to prepare.

Banana Custard Parfait

**Makes one serving
per banana**

❖ ❖ ❖ ❖ ❖ ❖ ❖ ❖ ❖ ❖ ❖

1 banana, just becoming overripe

Susan Wu of SuTao Café in Malvern, Pennsylvania invented this dish for the many customers who insisted that dessert just wouldn't be satisfying without dairy products. Here is a dessert that is all-natural, all-vegan, yet deliciously creamy. The texture of custard ice cream is achieved by the use of a horizontal juicer.

Preparation:

Peel the banana and freeze it overnight or for about 8 hours. Before the fruit begins to darken, run frozen banana through a horizontal juicer, such as the Champion. Serve in parfait glass topped with walnut bits or slivered almonds.

Bob's Peace Vigil Date Bars

Serves 8 or more

❖ ❖ ❖ ❖ ❖ ❖ ❖ ❖ ❖ ❖ ❖

20 ounces (about 4 cups) whole, pitted dates

1 cup whole pecans

½ cup shredded coconut

Bob's Peace Vigil Date Bars not only taste great; they are a wonderful source of energy and nutrients as well.

Preparation:
In a food processor, chop the pecans. Add dates and coconut; process until combined.

Press into an 8-by-8-by-2-inch baking tin, and cut into 2-inch squares.

Tips: Shredded coconut comes from the mature coconut; compared with the young coconut, it is richer in anti-bacterial oils. All forms of coconut provide organic iodine, nourishing the thyroid gland.

Pecans naturally contain monounsaturated fats which lower LDL (bad) cholesterol. Pecans also contain plant sterols, which support the immune system, as well as calcium, phosphorus, potassium, vitamin A, a variety of B-complex vitamins, and vitamin E; and they are an excellent source of zinc.

Dates contain a variety of B vitamins, and provide magnesium for healthy bone development. In proportion to weight, dates contain more potassium than do bananas. Potassium is an essential mineral needed to maintain the health of your nervous system and of proper muscle functions, including those of the heart. It also promotes efficient metabolism. Potassium is important for physically active people because potassium can be lost through perspiration.

We hope this convinces you that a bottle of water and a few of Bob's date bars will certainly support you on the path to world peace.

Traditional Salads and Dressings

Elegant and traditional, yet easy to make, these salads feature a variety of natural gems: fresh greens, fruits, nuts, pasta, beans – each graced with the perfect dressing.

Orange with Spinach and Romaine Lettuce

Walnut Pear Salad with Celery Seed Dressing

Sesame Green Bean Salad

Black Bean and Corn Salad

Pasta Salad

Zesty Orzo Salad

Salad with Fresh Herb Vinaigrette Dressing

Creamy Green Onion Dressing

Spiced Tahini Dressing

Orange with Spinach and Romaine Lettuce

Serves 6

❖ ❖ ❖ ❖ ❖ ❖ ❖ ❖ ❖ ❖ ❖ ❖ ❖

Bunch of spinach leaves

Bunch of romaine lettuce leaves

½ cup toasted, slivered almonds

2 cups Mandarin oranges
(11-ounce can, drained)

For the perfect salad dressing to complement this dish, combine the following in a blender:

½ cup olive oil

¼ cup cider vinegar

½ cup Florida Crystals natural sugar, less 1 tablespoon

½ medium onion, chopped

1 teaspoon celery seed

¾ teaspoon salt

½ clove garlic, minced

Oranges are rich in calcium, folate, potassium and vitamin C. Here is a delicious way to enjoy them.

Preparation:
Add dressing to lettuce and spinach leaves, mix in Mandarin oranges and top with slivered almonds.

Tip: This salad is a great source of calcium. Both almonds and green vegetables provide calcium that your body can readily absorb.

Walnut Pear Salad with Celery Seed Dressing

Serves 4

1 butterhead lettuce

1 to 2 halved, cored, unpeeled pears (such as Bosc or Asian Hosui), thinly sliced lengthwise

Coarsely chopped walnuts

Handful of dried cranberries

Bosc pears have a firm, dense, sweet-tasting flesh. Pears are ripe when they yield to gentle pressure at the stem end.

Preparation:
Cover the serving platter with lettuce. Then cover the lettuce layer with thinly sliced pears. Sprinkle with chopped walnuts and dried cranberries as desired.

Serve with the dressing for *Orange with Spinach and Romaine Lettuce* (previous recipe).

Sesame Green Bean Salad

Serves 4

❖ ❖ ❖ ❖ ❖ ❖ ❖ ❖ ❖ ❖ ❖

2 pounds green beans, trimmed

2 tablespoons toasted sesame seeds

2 tablespoons fresh lemon juice

1½ teaspoons olive oil

1 teaspoon sea salt (or more to taste)

Freshly ground pepper

This easy, fresh green bean salad is great for entertaining, and the toasted sesame seeds add a warm essence.

Preparation:
Bring a large pot of salted water to a boil. Add the green beans and cook for about 5 minutes, until just tender. Drain and rinse under cold water. Place in a bowl and toss with the sesame seeds, lemon juice, oil, salt, and pepper to taste.

Black Bean and Corn Salad

Makes 4–5 main-course servings

❖ ❖ ❖ ❖ ❖ ❖ ❖ ❖ ❖ ❖ ❖ ❖

Dressing:

⅓ cup freshly squeezed lime juice

½ cup cold-pressed, olive oil

1 garlic clove, minced

1 teaspoon fine sea salt

⅛ teaspoon cayenne pepper

Salad:

Two 15-ounce cans black beans, rinsed and drained

2 ears of corn, kernels cut off the cob, or 1½ cups frozen corn, thawed

1 avocado, peeled, stone removed, and cut into ½-inch pieces

1 small red bell pepper, seeded and cut into ½-inch pieces

2 medium tomatoes, cut into ½-inch pieces

6 green onions, with tops, finely chopped

1 fresh hot chile pepper, seeded and minced

½ cup coarsely chopped fresh cilantro (optional)

Lime juice lends pizzazz to this salad. Thanks to John Robbins, author of *May All Be Fed: Diet For A New World,* for sharing this recipe.

For the dressing, shake the lime juice, olive oil, garlic, salt, and cayenne pepper in a small covered jar until the ingredients are well mixed.

In a salad bowl, combine the canned beans, corn, avocado, bell pepper, tomatoes, green onions, chile pepper, and cilantro.

Shake the dressing again, and pour it over the salad. Stir to thoroughly coat the salad.

Tip: The salad can be prepared a few hours ahead, but don't add the avocado until serving time. Refrigerate, and adjust the seasoning before serving.

Pasta Salad

Serves 6

❖❖❖❖❖❖❖❖❖❖❖❖❖

1 pound dry macaroni, cooked *al dente*

About 9 cups in total of diced red pepper, chopped red onion or scallions (mostly the white parts), carrots, together with blanched broccoli, asparagus, and snap beans.

Mustard Vinaigrette Dressing:

1 tablespoon natural (grainy) Dijon mustard

4 tablespoons red wine or balsamic vinegar

½ cup cold-pressed, olive oil

1 or 2 minced cloves of garlic

½ teaspoon combined salt and ground pepper

Fresh, chopped herbs such as dill, parsley and basil

Chef Julia Child expressed a disinterest in pasta salads – doubtless having never tried this one. Fresh vegetables and lots of fresh herbs make this recipe a welcome guest at summer gatherings.

Preparation:
Combine all ingredients. Refrigerate, but let the dish stand at room temperature for a bit before serving.

Tip: See "The Art of Preparing a Perfect Pasta" (in the Classic Pasta Dishes section) for sound culinary counsel.

Zesty Orzo Salad

Serves 6 to 8

❖ ❖ ❖ ❖ ❖ ❖ ❖ ❖ ❖ ❖ ❖ ❖

Salad:

12 ounces dry orzo pasta, cooked, rinsed with cool water, and drained

½ cup red onion, diced

1 bunch scallions (mostly the white parts), chopped

6 or more sun-dried tomato halves, diced

½ red and ½ yellow bell pepper, diced

6 or more Spanish olives, pitted and chopped

4 artichoke hearts, chopped

1 can red kidney beans, rinsed and drained

½ cup cooked lima beans, fresh or frozen

¼ cup fresh parsley, minced

¼ cup fresh dill, minced

Sea salt

Ground pepper

Dressing:

½ cup extra virgin olive oil

⅓ cup wine vinegar

Juice of l lemon

Pinch of turmeric

Pinch of Florida Crystals natural sugar to taste

Orzo is a small, rice-shaped pasta enjoyed in salads and soups. Sun-dried tomatoes are a wonderful complement to orzo. This recipe celebrates the combination, and adds a few other delights from the garden. Abundanza!

Preparation:

Place cooked orzo in a salad bowl and stir in red onion, scallions, sun-dried tomatoes, bell peppers, olives, artichoke hearts, kidney beans, lima beans, parsley and dill. Season with salt and pepper to taste.

Whisk dressing ingredients to blend them; taste the dressing and adjust seasonings before combining it with the salad, stirring well. Serve slightly chilled.

Tip: Find information about *Florida Crystals* natural sugar in the Glossary's the *Key to Ingredients, Nutrients, and Vegetarian T erms.*

Salad with Fresh Herb Vinaigrette Dressing

Serves 6

Dressing:
(in addition to 10 cups of salad greens)

½ cup olive oil

2 tablespoons fresh lemon juice

2 tablespoons red wine vinegar

2 cloves garlic, minced

1 teaspoon Dijon mustard

2 teaspoons chopped fresh parsley

2 teaspoons chopped fresh basil

2 teaspoons chopped fresh tarragon

2 teaspoons chopped fresh chives

Fine sea salt

Ground pepper

A variety of salads makes for an attractive buffet, and this dressing takes advantage of the freshest herbs at the market.

Preparation:
Whisk all ingredients together, including salt and pepper to taste. Serve over 10 or more cups of salad greens. Add sliced tomatoes, red onion, and avocado.

Creamy Green Onion Dressing

Makes about 1¾ cups

7 scallions with tops, finely chopped

⅛ cup rice vinegar

⅛ cup tamari

1 cup Tofutti milk-free "Better than Sour Cream"

½ cup olive oil

¼ teaspoon salt

Ground pepper

This dressing is a rich and satisfying complement to a variety of greens.

Preparation:
Using a blender, mix all ingredients, including pepper to taste.

Tip: Please refer to the Glossary at the end of this book to find out about *Tofutti* vegan products and scallions too.

Spiced Tahini Dressing

Makes 1½ cups

½ cup tahini (sesame butter)

2 tablespoons olive oil

1 tablespoon tamari

2 teaspoons rice vinegar

½ cup fresh lemon juice

⅓ cup water

2 tablespoons fresh parsley

1 garlic clove, minced

Ground pepper

This rich dressing works wonders on a simple green salad.

Preparation:
Place all ingredients, including pepper to taste, into a blender; blend thoroughly. Refrigerate.

The Art of Preparing a Perfect Pasta

Use at least one quart of water for every four ounces of dry semolina pasta. If you skimp on water, there will not be enough to dilute the starch, and the pasta will have a soft coating and will not cook evenly.

Bring the pot of water to a rolling boil. Add 1½ heaping tablespoons of salt for every 4 quarts of water. Drop the pasta all at once into the boiling water, keeping the heat high. Cook the pasta, uncovered, at a fast boil. Don't hurry. Pasta added to water before it starts to boil turns out mushy and sticky. The water temperature drops when you add the pasta, but if you have a fast boil, the water should stay hot enough for proper cooking.

After you add the pasta to the boiling water, stir with a long wooden spoon to keep the noodles moving freely and cooking evenly.

Cooking *al dente* means preparing the pasta so that the noodles are tender but still firm, and it is the best way to do justice to your pasta. To be sure, remove a noodle from the pot and take a test bite. Do not procrastinate on this one; your noodles will continue to soften after your remove them from the stove and as you drain them.

Except when using thin or brothy sauces such as marinara, pasta needs to be moist to combine well. So drain it quickly, remove it from the colander and place it back in the cooking pan to keep warm, tossed with a little olive oil, or use warmed serving bowls. Then use a fork and spoon and quickly toss it with the sauce.

The Classic Mediterranean Salad with Mint offers a perfect salad and dressing to accompany any pasta dish; find it in the *Raw Delights* section of this book.

Main Dishes ❖ Classic Pasta Dishes

These outstanding pasta dishes connect us directly with the earth and its grains in the most wonderful way. We have more than one lasagne dish, and more than one pesto dish too. They are so good that we couldn't decide which to include, so we are offering them all, and you can decide. We hope you agree that each one is uniquely delicious, healthful, sumptuous, and gorgeous.

Penne with Asparagus Pesto

Cashew Cream Lasagne

Tofu Spinach Lasagne

Penne All'Arrabbiata with Olives

Priscilla's Presto Pesto

Spring Pasta with Carrots, Asparagus, and Pesto

Pasta, Green Beans and Potatoes with Pesto

Pasta with Artichoke Hearts

Linguine with Broccoli, Pine Nuts and Red Pepper Flakes

Lentil Orzo Casserole

Butternut Squash Sauce over Linguine

Spaghetti Primavera

Linguine with Cauliflower and Onions

Sauerkraut and Noodles

Penne with Asparagus Pesto

Serves 4

❖ ❖ ❖ ❖ ❖ ❖ ❖ ❖ ❖ ❖ ❖ ❖

1 pound dry penne pasta (small, plume-shaped tubes)

1 pound asparagus

¼ cup pine nuts

2 or 3 garlic cloves

½ teaspoon salt

½ cup olive oil

⅔ cup soy Parmesan cheese

Asparagus is one of the first vegetables ready for the traditional spring harvest. Here, it graces a dish of hot pasta.

Preparation:

Bring water to boil for pasta. Trim woody ends from asparagus. Cut stalks crosswise into 2-inch pieces, reserving tips. In a steamer, steam stalks over boiling water, covered, for 4 minutes. Add reserved asparagus tips and steam about 1 minute. Drain well, and pat dry.

In food processor, pulse pine nuts and garlic with salt until finely chopped. Add asparagus, oil and pulsed mix until asparagus is coarsely chopped. Transfer pesto to a large bowl and stir in soy Parmesan cheese. Cook the pasta, reserving a third of the cup of the cooking water, and drain the pasta. Add the pasta and reserved cooking water to the pesto, tossing to coat, and season with salt and pepper.

Tip: Please refer to the *Key to Ingredients, Nutrients, and Vegetarian Terms,* in the Glossary at the end of this book (under *cheese*) to find out about soy (vegan) Parmesan cheese.

Cashew Cream Lasagne

Serves 6 to 8

❖ ❖ ❖ ❖ ❖ ❖ ❖ ❖ ❖ ❖ ❖

5 cups Zucchini-Tomato Sauce for Pasta (under Kind Complements)

Béchamel Sauce (see below)

Tofu filling (see below)

1½ pounds of dried lasagne noodles

Béchamel Sauce:

4½ tablespoons olive oil

6 tablespoons flour

2½ cups soy milk (do not use nonfat)

1 clove garlic (quartered)

¼ teaspoon nutmeg

Sea salt

Ground pepper

Tofu filling:

2 cups of cashews

2 cloves of garlic

Two 12-ounce packages of silken tofu (such as the firm Mori-Nu variety)

Juice of half a lemon

1 tablespoon olive oil

2 teaspoons nutritional yeast

This lasagne has a rich, creamy and cheese-like filling; your guests might ask if it is really vegan. It can be assembled, covered with foil, and refrigerated several hours before baking.

Béchamel Sauce Preparation:

Warm soy milk in a small sauce pan. In a medium sauce pan, heat olive oil over low heat. Gradually whisk in flour, spoonful by spoonful. Continue to whisk for 2 minutes or so. Slowly pour in heated soy milk, whisking all the way. When mixture is smooth, add garlic, nutmeg, and salt and pepper to taste. Cook over low heat for about 20 minutes, stirring frequently until thick.

Tofu Filling Preparation:

Grind cashews and garlic finely in a blender or food processor. Add all other ingredients (gradually if using a blender; at once if using a food processor) and process until smooth. The mixture should have the consistency of ricotta cheese.

Boil lasagne noodles for 6 minutes in salted water. Be very careful to not let them stick. Rinse well in cold water after draining.

Heat oven to 350 degrees F. Spread a small amount of Zucchini-Tomato Sauce on the bottom of a large baking dish. Place a layer of noodles on top. Spread a thick layer of tofu filling on the noodles. Pour a layer of béchamel sauce and spread evenly over the filling. Spread Zucchini-Tomato Sauce over this and cover with another layer of noodles. Repeat steps until all of the ingredients are used and you can finish with a light layer of Zucchini-Tomato Sauce. Cover with foil and bake for about 45 minutes.

Increase oven temperature to 375 degrees F after 25 to 30 minutes of the overall baking time.

Tofu Spinach Lasagne

Serves 8 to 10

❖ ❖ ❖ ❖ ❖ ❖ ❖ ❖ ❖ ❖ ❖ ❖

12 lasagne noodles

1 tablespoon olive oil

6 cups marinara sauce

1½ pounds soft tofu, excess water removed

20 ounces frozen chopped spinach

1 large onion, minced

2 tablespoons fresh basil and oregano or 2 teaspoons dried herbs

¾ teaspoon salt

1 teaspoon minced garlic

This exciting and delicious "green" lasagne satisfies a craving for spinach, and it is beautiful to behold.

Preparation:
Cook and drain the spinach. Cook the noodles, adding oil to the boiling water. When the noodles are done, drain off most of the hot water and add cold water to the pot so that the noodles will be cool enough to handle. Set noodles aside.

To make filling, process in blender (in two or three batches) the tofu, spinach, herbs, onion, salt, and garlic. Lightly oil a lasagne pan.

Make layers in the following order: Sauce, noodles, filling. (The noodles will be easier to handle if you leave them in the cool water until you are ready to use them. Run your fingers along the length of each noodle to remove excess water before layering them in the pan.)

Repeat until the pan is full, finishing with a layer of noodles and sauce. Bake uncovered at 350 degrees F for 45 minutes.

Tips: Because the pasta is cooked twice – boiled first and then baked, pasta in lasagne dishes should boil until just flexible but still quite firm. To test, cut into a piece. Do rinse lasagne noodles after draining, to avoid tearing the noodles when separating them.

To cook the pasta ahead of time, boil the pasta just al dente. Drain, rinse under cold running water to stop the cooking, and again drain thoroughly. Let pasta cool completely, then brush lightly with olive oil to keep it from sticking. Pasta can be refrigerated in a covered bowl for up to three days.

Marinara sauce is described in the Glossary.

Penne All'Arrabbiata with Olives

Serves 6

❖ ❖ ❖ ❖ ❖ ❖ ❖ ❖ ❖ ❖

1 pound dry penne pasta

⅓ cup cold-pressed, olive oil

2 cups or more canned crushed tomatoes

Sea salt

1 clove minced garlic

2 tablespoons fresh parsley, minced

2 tablespoons dry white wine

1 tablespoon capers

¼ to ½ teaspoon red pepper flakes

1 cup chopped black olives

The Italian word arrabbiata denotes a tomato or bell pepper sauce, with an ample sprinkling of red pepper flakes.

Preparation:

Heat 2 tablespoons olive oil. Add tomatoes, and salt to taste. Cook over medium heat for 20 minutes, stirring frequently. In a large skillet, heat remaining olive oil and add garlic and parsley; deglaze with wine, and when evaporated, fold in the tomato sauce, capers, red pepper flakes and olives.

Cook the pasta. Toss with sauce over high heat for 1 minute; then transfer to serving platter.

Priscilla's Presto Pesto

Yields enough for
½ pound pasta

❖ ❖ ❖ ❖ ❖ ❖ ❖ ❖ ❖ ❖ ❖

⅓ cup pine nuts

1 cup loosely packed fresh basil leaves

2 mashed garlic cloves

¼–⅓ cup olive oil

Sea salt

Because Priscilla's mother, Marianna, always used fresh basil from the family gardens, homemade pesto sauce became a central feature in Priscilla's cooking from an early age. Commercially available pesto is difficult to find without cheese. Here is a pure basil and pine nut version and several recipes to demonstrate its versatility.

Preparation:

Put the nuts, basil, garlic, and oil in a blender. Purée until the mixture is well blended. Add salt to taste. Use immediately or store in a covered container in the refrigerator.

Spring Pasta with Carrots, Asparagus, and Pesto

Serves 2

❖ ❖ ❖ ❖ ❖ ❖ ❖ ❖ ❖ ❖ ❖

Pesto sauce (such as *Priscilla's Presto Pesto* in the previous recipe)

8 ounces dry penne pasta

½ pound asparagus, bottoms snapped off

2 carrots, cut into thick matchsticks

4 shallots, minced

1 tablespoon olive oil

Pinch of sea salt

Asparagus is a member of the lily family. About one-half cup of cooked asparagus contains about 20 calories, is a very good source of vitamin A, has 26 milligrams of vitamin C and fair amounts of riboflavin, thiamin and niacin (B vitamins). Cooked asparagus should be just tender – never mushy.

Preparation:

Boil 3 quarts of water and cook the pasta.

Warm the olive oil and add the carrots. Sauté for 1 minute, then add 1 to 2 tablespoons of water and simmer for 3 minutes, covered. Cut the asparagus into small pieces. Add the asparagus and shallots with another 2 tablespoons of water to the cooking carrots. Cover and cook for another 4 minutes. Cook off any excess water. Season to taste with salt. Add the vegetables to the pasta. Toss with pesto (see previous recipe).

Pasta, Green Beans and Potatoes with Pesto

Serves 4

❖ ❖ ❖ ❖ ❖ ❖ ❖ ❖ ❖ ❖ ❖

2 cups packed tender young basil leaves

⅓ cup pine nuts

1 teaspoon salt (plus 2 tablespoons to add to the cooking water)

2 large garlic cloves, minced

½ cup, extra-virgin olive oil

¼ cup grated soy Parmesan

½ pound small potatoes, peeled and cut into ¼-inch-thick slices

¼ pound tender young green beans, cut into 1-inch lengths

¾ to 1 pound thin spaghetti

Black pepper

Fresh pesto, pasta, green beans and potatoes make an excellent combination.

Preparation:

Make pesto by mixing basil, pine nuts, garlic, and the 1 teaspoon of salt in bowl of the food processor. Pulse until mixture is coarse and grainy. Pour olive oil into the food processor, and keep mixing. Add soy parmesan into the machine; process just enough to mix well.

Bring about six quarts water to rolling boil. Add two tablespoons salt and the potato slices. Cook for about 5 minutes, or until potatoes have started to soften but are not cooked through. Add green beans, and after 1 minute add the pasta. Stir and continue boiling for another 9 minutes.

When potatoes and beans are tender, drain and turn pasta and vegetables immediately into a heated bowl. Add pesto and mix thoroughly. Grind black pepper over top as desired and serve immediately.

Tip: Please refer to *Key to Ingredients, Nutrients, and Vegetarian Terms*, in the Glossary at the end of this book (under *cheese*), to find out about soy (vegan) Parmesan cheese.

Pasta with Artichoke Hearts

Serves 2 to 3

❖ ❖ ❖ ❖ ❖ ❖ ❖ ❖ ❖ ❖ ❖

Up to 1 pound (12 to 16 ounces) dry penne pasta

3 tablespoons cold-pressed, olive oil

2 to 3 shallots, chopped

2 cloves, minced garlic

2 or more sliced, fresh tomatoes

One 14-ounce can artichoke hearts, drained and cut in quarters

1 teaspoon dried basil

6 or more sun-dried tomatoes, chopped

¼ teaspoon crushed red pepper flakes

This recipe is bursting with superb flavor and character.

Preparation:

Cook pasta. In skillet sauté in olive oil, chopped shallots, minced garlic, sliced, chopped fresh tomatoes, and artichoke hearts. Add basil, sun-dried tomatoes, salt and pepper, and crushed red pepper flakes. Sauté for 12 to 15 minutes. Add to cooked pasta.

Linguine with Broccoli, Pine Nuts and Red Pepper Flakes

Serves 2 to 3

❖ ❖ ❖ ❖ ❖ ❖ ❖ ❖ ❖ ❖ ❖ ❖

1½ pounds broccoli, peeled, cut into florets, leaving about 1½ inches of stalk

½ to ⅔ pound dried linguine or farfalle pasta

5 tablespoons olive oil

2 medium garlic cloves, minced

½ cup chopped sun-dried tomatoes

⅛ to ¼ teaspoon dried red pepper flakes

Sea salt

Fresh ground pepper

¼ cup or more of pine nuts, lightly toasted

Sprinkle of grated soy Parmesan (optional)

Broccoli is a highly nutritious, versatile vegetable, and this wonderful recipe is quick and easy.

Preparation:

Blanch broccoli in large pot of boiling, salted water for about 3 minutes, until just crisp-tender. Drain and refresh under cold water. Drain well. Cook pasta in large pot of boiling water until just tender. Drain well. Meanwhile, heat oil in heavy, large skillet over medium-low heat. Add garlic and stir 1 minute. Add sun-dried tomatoes and pepper flakes to the skillet; stir 30 seconds. Add broccoli and stir about 2 minutes, until heated throughout. Add the pasta to the skillet and turn, to coat it with oil. Mix in soy Parmesan, if desired. Season generously with salt and pepper. Transfer the noodles to a heated platter. Sprinkle with pine nuts.

Lentil Orzo Casserole

Serves 4 to 6

❖ ❖ ❖ ❖ ❖ ❖ ❖ ❖ ❖ ❖ ❖

2 tablespoons cold-pressed, olive oil

2 medium onions, chopped

2 medium carrots, peeled and diced

6 medium cloves garlic, minced

Small pinch of red pepper flakes

1 cup dry brown lentils, rinsed

1 tablespoon chopped fresh thyme (or 1 teaspoon dried)

3 cups vegetable broth

6 ounces dry orzo pasta

One 14.5-ounce can diced tomatoes (fire-roasted if possible)

⅓ cup plain dry bread crumbs

2 tablespoons chopped fresh flat-leaf parsley

Canola-oil cooking spray

Lentils are an excellent source of iron. This recipe is an excellent winter dish.

Preparation:

In a large saucepan, heat 1 tablespoon oil over medium heat. Add onions and carrots; cook, stirring often, for 4 to 6 minutes until they soften. Add garlic and pepper flakes; cook, stirring, for 30 to 60 seconds. Add lentils and thyme; stir to coat. Add the broth and bring to a simmer. Reduce heat to low, cover and simmer for 25 minutes.

Preheat oven to 350 degrees F. Coat a deep, 3-quart casserole dish with cooking spray. Transfer lentil mixture to prepared casserole. Add pasta, tomatoes and salt and pepper to taste; mix with rubber spatula. Pour in 1¼ cups boiling water.

Cover with oven-proof lid and bake until lentils and orzo are almost tender, about 25 minutes. Uncover and stir to redistribute ingredients.

In a small bowl, mix together bread crumbs, parsley and the remaining 1 tablespoon oil. Bake, uncovered, for 15–20 additional minutes, until the casserole is bubbly and the top is crusty.

Butternut Squash Sauce over Linguine

Serves 3 to 4

❖ ❖ ❖ ❖ ❖ ❖ ❖ ❖ ❖ ❖ ❖

2 cloves garlic

Dashes of cold-pressed, olive oil

1 butternut squash

1 teaspoon dry vegetable broth seasoning

1 red bell pepper, chopped

Pinch red pepper flakes

12 ounces of dry linguine

This recipe was inspired from a dish I enjoyed in an Italian restaurant in South Norwalk, Connecticut.

Preparation:

Boil 3 quarts of water and cook linguine.

Sauté the garlic briefly in olive oil. Cut the squash in half and remove the seeds. Cook the squash, brushed with olive oil, face-down in a greased pan. Bake at 375 degrees F for 30 to 40 minutes. Mash the squash, adding about 1½ to 2 cups of hot water from the cooked pasta for consistency. Add a teaspoon or more of dried vegetable broth seasoning, a pinch of crushed red pepper flakes, and salt. Sauté the red bell pepper, softening it with the garlic mixture, and add it to the squash. Serve the mix over linguine.

Spaghetti Primavera

Serves 6

❖ ❖ ❖ ❖ ❖ ❖ ❖ ❖ ❖ ❖ ❖

1 pound spaghetti

7 tablespoons olive oil

1½ cups broccoli, coarsely chopped

1½ cups snow peas

1 cup sliced zucchini

1 cup baby peas

6 sliced asparagus

2 medium tomatoes, chopped

3 teaspoons minced garlic

¼ cup parsley, chopped

¼ cup pine nuts

10 mushrooms, sliced

1 cup non-dairy creamer

⅓ cup vegan margarine

⅓ cup fresh basil, chopped

Sea salt

Ground pepper

½ cup soy Parmesan cheese (optional)

"Primavera" means "spring" in Italian. When spring arrives, Italian cooks routinely add spring vegetables to pasta dishes. Here's a delightful variation of the original recipe without chicken stock or dairy products.

Preparation:

Cook spaghetti *al dente.*

Blanch broccoli, snow peas, zucchini, baby peas and asparagus in boiling water for 3 to 4 minutes. Rinse in cold water and set aside.

In medium skillet, heat 1 tablespoon olive oil. Add tomatoes 1 teaspoon garlic, parsley, salt and pepper to taste. Sauté for 2 to 3 minutes. Set the skillet mix aside, keeping it warm.

Toast pine nuts in the oven for a couple of minutes until they are lightly browned. Place them in a larger skillet with the remaining olive oil, garlic, mushrooms, and blanched vegetables. Simmer for a few minutes. Add spaghetti, soy creamer, margarine and basil (and soy Parmesan if desired). Mix gently with a fork.

Top with sautéed tomatoes and serve immediately.

Tip: Please refer to the *Key to Ingredients, Nutrients, and Vegetarian Terms,* in the Glossary at the end of this book (under *vegan margarine* and *cheese*), to find out about vegan margarines and a soy-based Parmesan alternative.

Linguine with Cauliflower and Onions

Serves 2 to 3

❖ ❖ ❖ ❖ ❖ ❖ ❖ ❖ ❖ ❖ ❖

12 ounces dry linguine, cooked

1 head of cauliflower

Cold-pressed, olive oil

1 large onion, Vidalia if possible

1 can (about 1 quart) plum tomatoes

Crushed red pepper flakes

Sea salt

Ground pepper

This is one of our favorite recipes, a delightful pasta entrée with splendid flavor.

Preparation:

Cut cauliflower into bite-sized florets. Sauté in several table-spoons of olive oil until lightly browned; then add the chopped onion and sauté the mix until the onion is transparent. Break tomatoes into the mixture and cook for about 20 minutes or more over medium heat, adding black pepper, salt and a pinch of crushed red pepper flakes. Serve over cooked linguine.

Variation: At time of simmering, add 2 cloves chopped garlic, slightly more tomato, 2 table-spoons pine nuts, and 2 tablespoons yellow raisins.

Sauerkraut and Noodles

Serves 6 to 8

❖ ❖ ❖ ❖ ❖ ❖ ❖ ❖ ❖ ❖ ❖

2 pounds sauerkraut from can or glass jar, such as Eden Organic, which comes in a 2-pound jar.

6 to 7 cups dry pasta noodles

1 tablespoon poppyseed

1 teaspoon salt

6 tablespoons vegan margarine

3 tablespoons olive oil

⅓ head of cabbage, cut into 1-inch squares

This delicious recipe was inspired by a classic Hungarian noodle dish.

Preparation:

Drain 2 pounds sauerkraut and squeeze the sauerkraut dry. Sauté until browned in a frying pan with 6 tablespoons vegan margarine. Turn out into a casserole dish. Cut cabbage into coarse, 1-inch squares and sauté in the same frying pan in 1 to 2 tablespoons of olive oil. Add cabbage to the sauerkraut.

Cook 6 to 7 cups of noodles in boiling water; drain and add them to the sauerkraut and cabbage. Add 1 tablespoon poppyseed and about 1 teaspoon salt. Add 1 tablespoon olive oil. Cover with foil and reheat in oven before serving. Serve with Apple Sauce Sweetened with Agave Nectar (recipe under *Kind Complements*).

Tip: Please refer to the *Key to Ingredients, Nutrients, and Vegetarian Terms,* in the Glossary at the end of this book (under *vegan margarine*) for some words to the wise about vegan margarine.

Main Dishes ❖ *Hearty and Timeless*

Fill your home with memories. These dishes will warm your table, fill your kitchen with inspiring aromas, and linger in your thoughts far longer than they linger in the pot.

Ellie's Arroz y Habichuelas (Puerto Rican Rice and Beans)

Italian Vegetable and Potato Stew

Vegetarian Chili

Ratatouille

Melanzane alla Priscilla

Risotto with Spinach

Ellie's Arroz y Habichuelas (Puerto Rican Rice and Beans)

Serves 6 to 8

❖ ❖ ❖ ❖ ❖ ❖ ❖ ❖ ❖ ❖ ❖ ❖

1 pound package dry red kidney beans or small red beans ("habichuelas")

1 onion, sliced in rings

4 cloves of garlic, minced

¼ teaspoon oregano

¼ teaspoon black pepper

4 teaspoons salt

3 sprigs fresh coriander (also sold as cilantro or recao) leaves and cut stems, removing roots (if none of those are available, use 3 tablespoons dried coriander flakes)

1 cup (one 8-ounce can) tomato sauce

Canola oil

About 5 small sweet Puerto Rican peppers, called ajies dulces (or small sweet Mexican peppers)

2 cups white rice

Dash of hot sauce as desired

Friends of Animals member Ellie Maldonado, who lives in New York City, learned to cook this traditional dish decades ago. Its tangy sofrito sauce will inspire many a recipe request as it provides a hearty and delicious meal.

Preparation:

Beans: Put dried beans in a colander and wash thoroughly with cold running water, and then place them in 2 quarts (8 cups) of cold water for about 8 hours to soften. Wash the beans again carefully; drain and place beans in 3 quarts (12 cups) cold water in a 6-quart pot. Add the salt, and heat to a full boil for about 15 minutes. Reduce heat to boil gently in the pot, uncovered, for at least 1 hour, or until beans are tender but not mushy. Then, carefully pour out any remaining liquid that puts the water mark higher than 1 inch.

Sofrito: Line a frying pan with just enough canola oil to cover the surface, and slightly brown onion rings over medium heat. Add chopped garlic, black pepper and oregano, and the sliced Puerto Rican ajies dulces (sweet but strong red and green peppers) or Mexican sweet peppers (these come in pint packages in lovely hues of yellow, orange, and red). Then stir 8 ounces of tomato sauce into mixture. Raise heat slightly and allow tomato sauce to thicken with ingredients, add the cilantro to the sofrito mixture, and stir frequently as the mix thickens. Then add the sofrito to the pot of cooked beans. Reduce heat and continue to simmer for about 10 minutes. The dish is ready when sauce thickens to a slightly creamy consistency.

Rice: In a 2-quart pan, add 3 cups cold water to 2 cups dry rice. Cook

(Continued)

over medium-high heat until rice reaches a full boil. Then reduce heat to medium-low, and cover pan; allow rice to simmer until water is absorbed and rice grains are cooked. Fluff with a fork.

Serve beans with the preferred amount of rice, adding a few drops of hot pepper sauce to the beans if desired. Add a side dish of sliced avocados, seasoned with oil, lemon juice, and thinly sliced onion to taste.

Italian Vegetable and Potato Stew

Serves 6

1 large eggplant, peeled and cut into ½-inch cubes

1 teaspoon fine sea salt

3 tablespoons, cold-pressed olive oil, or more as needed

1 medium onion, chopped

2 stalks of celery, with leaves, chopped

1 green bell pepper, seeded and chopped

3 to 5 carrots, chopped

2 garlic cloves, minced

3 medium boiler potatoes, cut into ½-inch slices

28-ounce can unsweetened tomatoes in purée

1 cup vegetable bouillon or water

⅛ teaspoon crushed red pepper flakes

½ cup chopped fresh basil or 1 teaspoon dried basil

1 cup Mediterranean black olives, pitted and chopped

This stew is adapted from a recipe by John Robbins, author of *May All Be Fed: Diet For A New World.*

Preparation:

Place the eggplant in a colander and toss with 1 teaspoon of the salt. Let it stand for 1 hour to draw out the bitter juices. Rinse well, drain, and pat it dry with a kitchen towel.

Heat 2 tablespoons of the oil in a large saucepan over medium heat. Add the eggplant and cook for about 4 minutes, stirring often, until lightly browned. You may have to add a little more oil if the eggplant sticks. Transfer to a plate and set aside.

Heat the remaining tablespoon of oil in the pan, and add the onion, celery, bell pepper, and garlic. Cook for about 5 minutes, stirring often, until softened.

Stir in the reserved eggplant, the potatoes, carrots, the tomatoes with their purée, vegetable bouillon, the remaining ½ teaspoon salt, and the red pepper flakes; if using dried basil, add it now. Bring to a simmer, then reduce the heat to low, cover, and simmer for 45 minutes to 1 hour, stirring occasionally, until the potatoes are tender.

Stir in the olives and, if using, the fresh basil, continue cooking for about 5 minutes to blend in the leaves' essence. Serve the stew hot, warm, or at room temperature.

Vegetarian Chili

Serves 8

Two 16-ounce cans kidney beans, rinsed and drained; or a combination of pinto and black beans

2 tablespoons olive oil

1 medium onion, coarsely chopped

2 medium carrots, finely chopped

2 ribs celery, with leaves, finely chopped

1 medium green bell pepper, seeded and chopped.

3 garlic cloves, minced

2 tablespoons chili powder

2 teaspoons ground cumin

2 teaspoons dried oregano

2 bay leaves

1 teaspoon salt

$\frac{1}{8}$ teaspoon cayenne pepper, or more to taste

16-ounce can tomato sauce

2 medium tomatoes or one 14-ounce can unsweetened Italian tomatoes, coarsely chopped

1 cup vegetable broth

3 fresh Serrano peppers, diced

1 cup cashews

This one is a great candidate for any cook-off. If you enjoy intense heat, try adding one habanero pepper instead of the Serrano pepper.

Preparation:

In a large pot, heat the olive oil over medium heat. Add the onion, carrots, celery, bell pepper, garlic, and chili peppers, cover, and cook for about 7 minutes, stirring occasionally, until softened. Add the chili powder, cumin, oregano, bay leaves, salt, and pepper, and stir for 30 seconds. Stir in the beans, tomato sauce, tomatoes, vegetable broth and peppers. Cook partially covered, until thickened about 20 minutes. Stir in the cashews and cook for 5 minutes or until heated thoroughly. Remove the bay leaves and serve immediately.

Ratatouille

Serves 4

6 tablespoons olive oil

3 cloves garlic, chopped

2 green or red peppers cut into wide strips

1½ cups shallots (or white parts of scallions), chopped

Medium eggplant, peeled and cut into 1-inch cubes; or 2 small ones, sliced

4 tomatoes, chopped

2 zucchini squashes (about 1 pound), sliced

½ teaspoon basil

¼ teaspoon thyme

¼ teaspoon marjoram

Pinch of rosemary

1 teaspoon salt

Ground pepper

This famous preparation is world-renowned, with variations aplenty throughout the Mediterranean. Even though many people think of ratatouille as the quintessential Provençal dish, ratatouille is actually a relatively modern invention, following the introduction of the tomato to Europe in the 1500s. (Read more about the versatile tomato under Zucchini-Tomato Sauce for Pasta in the section *Kind Complements.*)

Preparation:

Sprinkle salt over the cubes of eggplant and place them in a colander to drain for 1 hour. Gently press out excess moisture with paper towel.

Heat 4 tablespoons olive oil in large skillet, and add the eggplant and zucchini squash, cooking for 10 to 12 minutes until vegetables are golden and barely tender.

Remove eggplant and zucchini squash, reduce the heat, and in the same pan add 2 tablespoons olive oil, and cook shallots until slightly softened. Then add peppers and garlic, cooking and stirring occasionally for 8 to 12 minutes, until the vegetables are barely tender but not browned.

Season with salt, and the pepper to taste. Add tomatoes, basil, thyme, marjoram and rosemary. Reduce the heat to low; cover and cook for 5 minutes. Add the eggplant and zucchini squash, and cook until everything is tender, about 20 minutes.

Serve with brown rice.

Melanzane alla Priscilla

Serves 4 to 6

❖ ❖ ❖ ❖ ❖ ❖ ❖ ❖ ❖ ❖ ❖ ❖ ❖

2 medium, ripe eggplant, sliced

Whole-wheat flour

Olive oil

One quart "Zucchini-Tomato Sauce for Pasta" (under *Kind Complements*)

Large onion, chopped in semi-circles

Yellow bell pepper, chopped

3 to 4 small yellow squashes, sliced

1 chopped jalapeño pepper

When eggplant is cooked properly, it melts in the mouth. If preferred, substitute two small-to-medium white potatoes for the yellow squash.

Preparation:

Slice the eggplant horizontally (rather than in vertical strips), so that it is cut into rounds, each about a half-inch thick. Sprinkle the slices with salt and leave them for 20 to 30 minutes. The salt will draw out some of the water so your slices won't be too juicy when you cook them. After 30 minutes, press the slices with your hand and blot with towels.

Dredge each slice in whole-wheat flour, then fry the floured slices on both sides in a little olive oil. Keep the heat under the frying pan fairly high, and the slices won't absorb as much oil. Sauté the slices until they're lightly browned.

Lightly sauté onion, yellow pepper, squash and jalapeño pepper in a little olive oil for a few minutes.

Arrange half of the eggplant rounds in a large casserole dish. Cover them with half of the sautéed onions, yellow pepper, yellow squash and jalapeño pepper mixture. Repeat the layering with the remaining half of eggplant slices and other vegetable mixture.

Spread the casserole with Zucchini-Tomato Sauce.

Bake in a 350 degrees F oven for about 40 minutes or more.

Risotto with Spinach

Serves 4

6 cups vegetable broth

3 tablespoons extra-virgin, olive oil

½ finely chopped yellow onion

1 or 2 cloves garlic, crushed

¾ pound spinach, stemmed and thinly sliced crosswise

2 cups Arborio risotto rice

⅔ cup dry white wine

2 tablespoons vegan margarine

The technique for making risotto probably came from trying to cook the rice as a – *puls* (similar to porridge) – boiling it in milk, water, or broth until soft. In fact, a sort of rice porridge cooked in milk and sugar, *rixo in bona manera* ("rice in a good manner"), was documented in Venice since the fourteenth century.

Risotto is a very simple and nutritious dish, and easy to prepare. There are hundreds of types of Risotto, varying from the flavoring ingredient used; but in all the recipes you will need four basic components: *soffritto* (sautéed vegetables), broth, flavoring ingredients, and Italian rice. Serve with salad and crusty bread.

Preparation:
Bring broth to a simmer in a small saucepan over a medium heat; maintain simmer over low heat. In a large, heavy saucepan, warm oil over medium heat. Add onion and garlic; sauté for about 4 minutes, until softened. Add spinach, reduce heat to low; cover and cook for about 5 minutes, until tender; then transfer to a bowl using a slotted spoon, and set aside.

Add rice to pan; stir the rice for about 3 minutes, until grains are well coated with oil, translucent, with a white dot in the centers. Add wine and stir until absorbed.

Add broth a ladleful at a time, stirring frequently, after each addition. Wait until stock is almost completely absorbed before adding more. Reserve ¼ cup broth to add at the end.

After about 18 minutes, when the rice is almost tender to the bite but slightly firm in the center and looks creamy, add the spinach mixture to pan and add a ladleful of stock. Cook for 2 to 3 minutes, stirring occasionally, until spinach mixture is heated through and rice is al dente.

Remove from heat; stir in vegan margarine and reserved ¼ cup stock. Season with salt and pepper.

Main Dishes ❖ Enchanting Innovations

Celebrate the earth's gifts. Awaken your senses by trying a new path each day. And then invite your friends to experience a new recipe for dinner. Each of these dishes is as unique and special as they are.

Tempeh London Broil

Holiday Cashew Nut Roast

Baked Aubergine

Grilled Tofu with Mustard Dipping Sauce

Stuffed Bell Peppers with Tofu and Vegetables

Unchick'n Strips Sauté

Blackened Tempeh with Roasted Red Pepper Sauce

Roasted Red Pepper Sauce

Tempeh London Broil

Serves 8

❖ ❖ ❖ ❖ ❖ ❖ ❖ ❖ ❖ ❖ ❖ ❖

½ cup virgin olive oil

½ cup freshly squeezed lemon juice

½ cup tamari

2 cups white wine

Sea salt

Ground pepper

Four 8-ounce packages of tempeh, cut into 1-inch cubes

1 large Vidalia or white onion, chopped

2 medium zucchini squash, sliced

This main dish is a crowd-pleaser. It is best accompanied with Mashed Yukon Potatoes and a green salad.

Preparation:
In a bowl, prepare a marinade by combining the olive oil, lemon juice, tamari, wine, and salt and pepper to taste. Add tempeh.

Cover and place in refrigerator to marinate overnight; the tempeh will puff up as it absorbs the marinade.

Drain tempeh, reserving marinade.

Heat frying pan over medium to low heat. Add tempeh and small amount of the marinade to pan and cook for about 10 minutes, until it begins to brown. Add onion and zucchini.

Gradually stir in the rest of marinade. Continue cooking until tempeh is golden brown.

Holiday Cashew Nut Roast

Serves 4 to 6

❖ ❖ ❖ ❖ ❖ ❖ ❖ ❖ ❖ ❖ ❖ ❖

2 cups cashew pieces

4 ounces of brown rice

6 ounces of rye toast crumbs – including caraway seeds, or a dash of celery seed.

1 medium onion, chopped

2 cloves garlic, minced

2 large, ripe tomatoes

6 tablespoons olive oil

2 teaspoons brewer's yeast

½ teaspoon dried basil

½ teaspoon dried thyme

½ teaspoon of lemon juice (preferably freshly squeezed)

¼–½ cup vegetable broth

Dash of ground pepper

With a taste that reminds us of a delightful nut-based holiday stuffing, this is a fine addition to a festive buffet. Thanks to Robin Lane, co-founder of the annual London Vegan Festival, for this recipe.

Preparation:
Cook rice until tender; coarsley grind cashews. (This can easily be done by hand by carefully running a rolling pin or jar over bagged nuts.)

Chop onion and garlic finely and heat in oil until they are slightly brown; chop and add one of the tomatoes; simmer until soft.

Combine all of the ingredients and press into two 9-by-5-by-2½ -inch loaf pans or glass round pie baking dishes. Slice second tomato and use to decorate top of roasts (adding a small amount of olive oil to each tomato slice if desired).

Bake for 30 minutes or more at 350 degrees F.

Baked Aubergine

Ingredient

❖ ❖ ❖ ❖ ❖ ❖ ❖ ❖ ❖ ❖ ❖

1 large eggplant

Here's how to enjoy Cashew Nut Roast the next day (if there is any left).

Preparation:
Slice large eggplant in half lengthwise from stem to base and carve out hollows in each half. Rub olive oil over the halves, inside and out.

Stuff with the extra Cashew Nut Roast. Place in glass pie plate and top off generously with a simple tomato sauce, and dashes of red wine on each side. Sprinkle bread crumbs liberally over the top.

Bake at 400 degrees F until the sauce begins to brown slightly at the edge of the pie plate, and the eggplant feels soft when a knife is inserted.

Grilled Tofu with Mustard Dipping Sauce

Serves 4

❖ ❖ ❖ ❖ ❖ ❖ ❖ ❖ ❖ ❖ ❖

1 pound firm tofu

¼ cup, cold-pressed olive oil

1 lime, squeezed

¼ cup tamari

1 teaspoon minced fresh ginger, or ¼ teaspoon powdered ginger

1 clove minced garlic

Dash of cayenne pepper

Mustard Dipping Sauce (optional; recipe follows)

1½ tablespoons Dijon mustard

½ tablespoon brown rice vinegar

1½ tablespoons tamari

1 tablespoon fresh lemon juice

This uncommon recipe is especially helpful as an introduction to people who are new to soy products.

Preparation:
Cut tofu lengthwise into four filets. Mix together olive oil, lime juice, tamari, ginger, garlic and cayenne pepper. Marinate tofu in mixture for at least four hours or overnight.

Grill tofu over hot coals or on a stove top grill until heated through and lightly browned (3½ minutes each side).

Mustard Dipping Sauce:
Mix all ingredients in a small bowl and serve alongside tofu.

Orange with Spinach & Romaine Lettuce ❖ Spring Pasta with Carrots, Asparagus & Pesto ❖ Pages 48 & 63

Stuffed Bell Peppers with Tofu and Vegetables ❖ Page 85

Medley of Roasted Potatoes, Onions and Zucchini ❖ Page 91

Banana Almond Bread ❖ Cranberry Nut Bread ❖ Pages 100 & 102

Fresh Ginger Cake ❖ Page 117

Chocolate Marble Cheescake ❖ Page 134

Stuffed Bell Peppers with Tofu and Vegetables

Serves 2

❖ ❖ ❖ ❖ ❖ ❖ ❖ ❖ ❖ ❖ ❖

2 large red bell peppers

Olive oil for sautéing

1 large onion, finely chopped

3 cloves garlic, minced

1 small bunch basil, finely chopped

½ pound tofu, finely chopped

2 Roma tomatoes (Italian plum tomatoes), diced

2 teaspoons tamari or soy sauce

½ cup dry white wine

½ cup or more of cooked orzo

A pinch of red pepper flakes

A pinch of salt

Freshly cracked black pepper

The hearty filling gives peppers and other vegetables the central place in the meal. The alcohol in the wine is cooked off, but the rich essence of the grapes remains.

Preparation:

Cook orzo al dente, drain and set aside. Heat the oven to 375 degrees F.

Remove the tops of the peppers and scoop out the seeds. Rinse and set the peppers aside, reserving the tops.

In medium sauté pan or skillet, heat a small amount of olive oil. Add the onion, cover, and cook the onion until it is soft and translucent. Add the garlic, basil, tofu and tomatoes. Sauté to thoroughly heat the ingredients. Stir in the tamari and season with salt, pepper, and red pepper flakes to taste.

Add the cooked orzo.

Arrange the peppers on a well-greased pie plate. Fill each hollow with the tofu mixture. Pour white wine over the vegetables, and cap the peppers with their tops. Bake for about 25 to 30 minutes, or until the peppers are tender.

Unchick'n Strips Sauté

Serves 2

❖ ❖ ❖ ❖ ❖ ❖ ❖ ❖ ❖ ❖ ❖

One 6-ounce packet of vegan Lightlife "Smart Menu"™ Chick'n Strips

1 small chopped red pepper

6 chopped scallions (mainly the white parts), or 2 chopped shallots

One or more yellow squash, sliced

A handful of broccoli florets

Extra-virgin, cold-pressed olive oil

Tamari

1 tablespoon of freshly grated ginger

Pinch of sea salt

Pinch ground pepper

Pinch of paprika

Sprinkles of crushed red pepper flakes

Served with Jasmine rice, this is a quick and appealing dish, especially for those who are just making the switch from non-vegetarian foods. Some call this type of dish a mock meat, or a meat analogue. We'd suggest, however, that the taste, texture, and spices of good vegetarian meals are the real thing – not the other way round.

Preparation:
Sauté everything except for the strips in olive oil for about 10 minutes. Add strips sprinkled with paprika; add broccoli and cook at medium heat for about 4 to 5 minutes, stirring until golden brown. Add two tablespoons tamari and the crushed red pepper flakes. Stir and serve.

Tip: Please refer to the *Key to Ingredients, Nutrients, and Vegetarian Terms*, in the Glossary at the end of this book (under *Lightlife*) for some words to the wise about the Lightlife product line.

Blackened Tempeh with Roasted Red Pepper Sauce

Serves 2 to 3

❖ ❖ ❖ ❖ ❖ ❖ ❖ ❖ ❖ ❖ ❖

One 8-ounce package tempeh

1 tablespoon of olive oil

3 cups flour

2 tablespoons ground cumin

2 tablespoons dried herb mix
(such as basil and oregano)

3 tablespoons paprika

1 tablespoon chili powder

Pinch of sea salt

Pinch of ground pepper

1 tablespoon crushed red pepper
flakes

½ teaspoon cayenne pepper

Marinade:

12 ounces fresh salsa (see our
Fiery Salsa recipe in the Raw
Delights section)

1 cup white wine

½ tablespoon garlic

1 cup water

½ cup tamari or soy sauce

Our gratitude goes to Chef Mark Shadle for sharing this superb recipe, as well as the Roasted Red Pepper Sauce in the next recipe. Both recipes made their first appearance together in *It's Only Natural: Classic Vegan Recipes.* Please be careful to turn on your exhaust fan, or open a window when preparing Blackened Tempeh. Always use extreme caution when working with hot oils. Keep a lid that fits pan nearby in case pan flares up. Don't allow children, dogs, cats, or litigious friends near the stove.

Preparation:

Cut tempeh into thirds. Cut each third in half diagonally to form triangles. Cut each triangle in half through the middle, as though cutting through a cake round when making a layer cake. Use the above marinade to soak tempeh for at least six hours, preferably overnight.

Remove tempeh from marinade and press in the seasoning mix of flour, herbs, and spices.

Fry in hot pan with only one tablespoon of olive oil. A cast-iron skillet works best. Serve with Roasted Red Pepper Sauce (following recipe).

Roasted Red Pepper Sauce

Yields 4 cups

❖ ❖ ❖ ❖ ❖ ❖ ❖ ❖ ❖ ❖ ❖

2 tablespoons olive oil

2 cups roasted red peppers (sold in jars)

1 cup onion, diced

1 tablespoon garlic, minced

½ cup water

2 cups peach juice

⅓ cup brown rice syrup

2 tablespoons arrowroot mixed into 2 tablespoons of water

This piquant sauce accompanies the Blackened Tempeh in the previous recipe. Open new pepper jars just before you make this sauce for optimum freshness.

Preparation:

Sauté onions and garlic together in olive oil. Add peppers, water, rice syrup, and juice. Use a hand blender to purée. Bring to a boil with arrowroot and water.

Kind Complements ❖ Irresistible Side Dishes and Condiments

A rich gravy, a hearty vegetable medley, or a sweet touch of agave nectar: The right side dishes and condiments make a meal into an event. At your fingertips are the keys to classics with a zing.

Zucchini-Tomato Sauce for Pasta

Medley of Roasted Potatoes, Onions and Zucchini

Braised Brussels Sprouts with Lemon

Green Beans with Almonds

Spiced Orange Broccoli

Potato and Carrot au Gratin

Mashed Sweet Potatoes

Mashed Yukon Potatoes

Seasoned Vegetables with Butternut Squash

Miso Gravy

Apple Sauce Sweetened with Agave Nectar

Zucchini-Tomato Sauce for Pasta

Makes about 3 quarts

❖ ❖ ❖ ❖ ❖ ❖ ❖ ❖ ❖ ❖ ❖ ❖

1 large onion, chopped (Vidalia onion if possible)

1 clove garlic, minced

1 pound zucchini, trimmed and finely chopped in food processor

¼ cup olive oil

5 large, ripe tomatoes, chopped, or 2 (two) 28-ounce cans whole peeled tomatoes

2 teaspoons dried basil

1½ teaspoons salt

¼ teaspoon pepper

One 6-ounce can tomato paste

1 to 2 teaspoons of Florida Crystals natural sugar

Zucchini comes from the Italian plural of *zucchino,* a diminutive of *zucco,* from late Latin *cucutia,* from *cucurbita,* or "edible gourd" (compare the Sanskrit *carbhatah,* "cucumber"). The zucchini is the name given in North America for the green squash; and the word *squash,* in turn, is a Native American term, from Narraganset *askutasquash,* meaning "a green vegetable eaten green" or young.[7]

We usually associate tomatoes with Mediterranean cuisine, but they originated in the coastal highlands of western South America and appeared later in Central America where the Mayans used them as food. In the 1500s, conquistadores carried tomatoes eastward to Europe. Although Europeans at first believed tomatoes to be poisonous, Europeans eventually found many culinary uses for them; George Washington Carver shattered the myth and popularized them in North America. In 1893, the U.S. Supreme Court declared that the tomato was a vegetable. By the early 1900s, tomatoes had become a staple of North American culinary arts and home gardens.

Preparation:

Sauté onion, garlic, and zucchini in oil until soft; stir in tomatoes, basil, salt, pepper, and sugar. Add paste. Heat to bubbling; simmer for 30 minutes, or until sauce thickens.

Tip: Find information about *Florida Crystals* natural sugar in the Glossary's the *Key to Ingredients, Nutrients, and Vegetarian Terms.*

---

7 "Courgette: On the Nomenclature of Certain Cucurbitaceous Plants" – Faculty of Humanities, University of Copenhagen, http://www.hum.ku.dk/ami/courgette.html.

Medley of Roasted Potatoes, Onions and Zucchini

Serves 4–6

❖❖❖❖❖❖❖❖❖❖❖

3 pounds red potatoes, quartered

2 onions, cut into quarters or smaller

1 zucchini, chopped

2 tablespoons olive oil

3 tablespoons chopped fresh parsley or 1 tablespoon dried

3 tablespoons chopped fresh basil or 1 tablespoon dried

Sea salt

Ground pepper

This side dish, featuring red-skinned potatoes, can be prepared quickly. Most of the work is delegated to your oven.

Preparation:

Heat oven to 400 degrees F. Combine all ingredients in large bowl. Transfer to a roasting pan and bake for 40 to 50 minutes, until vegetables are golden brown. Stir vegetables several times during cooking to ensure even browning.

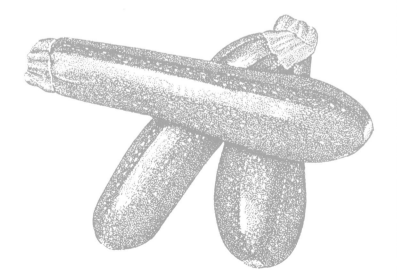

Braised Brussels Sprouts with Lemon

Serves 2 to 4

❖ ❖ ❖ ❖ ❖ ❖ ❖ ❖ ❖ ❖ ❖

12 Brussels sprouts

3 tablespoons vegan margarine

2 cloves garlic, crushed

¼ to ½ cup water

½ lemon or more for squeezing

Sea salt

Ground pepper

Do you know someone who hasn't given sprouts a chance? Urge them to hold off any final decisions until they try these nutty-sweet cabbages.

Preparation:
Rinse Brussels sprouts, pat them dry, and slice in halves, length-wise. With the tip of a paring knife, cut an "X" into the cut side of each sprout.

Warm the margarine in a medium skillet over medium-low heat. Add garlic and cook, stirring, until golden. Place the sprouts cut-side down in the garlic oil. Add water, cover, and cook for 15 to 20 minutes over low heat, until tender. Arrange on a warm platter and sprinkle lightly with lemon juice. Season with salt and pepper as desired.

Green Beans with Almonds

Serves 4

❖ ❖ ❖ ❖ ❖ ❖ ❖ ❖ ❖ ❖ ❖

1 pound green beans, trimmed

1 tablespoon vegan margarine

¼ to ½ cup sliced almonds

Sea salt

This side dish is always served at our Thanksgiving buffet, and it's always heartily welcomed. The beans have an energetic spring to them, and sliced almonds lend a gently smoky allure.

Preparation:
Cook beans in lightly salted boiling water about 3 minutes, until barely tender. Meanwhile, heat the vegan margarine over medium-low heat and add the almonds; cook, stirring, until barely browned. Drain the beans and mix with the almonds and margarine. Salt to taste.

Tip: Please refer to the *Key to Ingredients, Nutrients, and Vegetarian Terms,* in the Glossary at the end of this book (under *vegan margarine*) for some words to the wise about vegan margarine.

Spiced Orange Broccoli

Serves 4

❖ ❖ ❖ ❖ ❖ ❖ ❖ ❖ ❖ ❖ ❖

2 tablespoons olive oil

2 cloves garlic, minced

1 tablespoon minced shallot

Rind of 1 orange, chopped

⅛ teaspoon red pepper flakes

1 large bunch broccoli florets, cut into uniform pieces

⅓ cup orange juice

1 teaspoon balsamic vinegar

¼ teaspoon salt

¼ teaspoon toasted sesame oil

A member of the cabbage family and a close relative of cauliflower, broccoli offers one of the highest nutrient-to-calorie ration of any popular vegetable. A hint of pepper and citrus gives this broccoli dish an appealing glow.

Preparation:
Sauté first five ingredients in large frying pan over medium heat until garlic and shallots have softened, stirring frequently.

Add broccoli to pan; cook and stir 1 minute. Add orange juice, vinegar and salt. Cover and steam for 3 to 4 minutes over medium-high heat. Drizzle with sesame oil. Toss and serve hot.

Potato and Carrot au Gratin

Serves 6

❖ ❖ ❖ ❖ ❖ ❖ ❖ ❖ ❖ ❖ ❖ ❖

2 pounds Yukon Gold potatoes, peeled and very thinly sliced

1 teaspoon salt

½ teaspoon freshly ground pepper

¾ teaspoon to 1 teaspoon of dried basil

Medium onion, finely chopped

4 medium carrots, very thinly sliced

1 to 1½ cups vegetable broth

The Yukon Gold was the first Canadian-bred potato to be marketed and promoted by name. In this casserole it's paired with carrots, irresistibly browned and seasoned.

Preparation:

Heat oven to 400 degrees F with rack positioned in upper third of oven. Coat a shallow 2½ or 3-quart casserole with canola-oil cooking spray.

Pat potatoes dry with paper towels. Arrange half the potato slices in single layer over the bottom of the prepared casserole, overlapping them slightly. Season with a little salt, pepper and basil. Sprinkle with half the chopped onion.

Add all carrot slices, overlapping them slightly. Season with a little salt, pepper and basil; sprinkle with the remaining onion. Top with the remaining potato slices, overlapping them slightly. Season with the remaining salt, pepper and basil.

Add enough broth to come three-quarters of the way up vegetables. Cover casserole with lid and bake for 30 to 40 minutes, until potatoes are almost tender. Uncover and bake about 25 minutes more, until potatoes are fully tender.

Mashed Sweet Potatoes

Serves 4 to 6

❖ ❖ ❖ ❖ ❖ ❖ ❖ ❖ ❖ ❖

6 cups peeled and diced sweet potatoes

4 tablespoons vegan margarine

½ cup orange juice

3 tablespoons sliced almonds, toasted

Dash of salt

The sweet potato belongs to the same family of plants as the morning glory. Native to Central America, they have been cultivated in Southern United States since the 16th century. In this simple yet stylish dish, the potatoes' sweetness is accented by a touch of orange juice. The finishing touch is a sprinkling of toasted almonds.

Preparation:
Cook sweet potatoes through in boiling water. Mash with margarine. Add orange juice and salt. Serve topped with toasted nuts.

Tip: Please refer to the *Key to Ingredients, Nutrients, and Vegetarian Terms,* in the Glossary at the end of this book (under *vegan margarine*) for some words to the wise about vegan margarine.

Mashed Yukon Potatoes

Serves 4 to 6

❖ ❖ ❖ ❖ ❖ ❖ ❖ ❖ ❖ ❖

2 pounds Yukon or russet potatoes

¾ cup (or more) soy creamer, heated

4 tablespoons vegan margarine, melted

½ cup chopped fresh chives or 1 teaspoon each dried dill and parsley

Sea salt

Ground pepper

If anyone you know loved to serve home-style mashed potatoes at holiday gatherings, these fluffy mashed potatoes are likely to bring back warm memories. If desired, use plain soy milk in place of soy creamer.

Preparation:
Bring large pot of water to boil to cook the potatoes until tender. Drain and peel the potatoes and transfer them to a large bowl. Add the hot soy milk creamer and melted margarine. Using an electric mixer, beat the mixture until smooth. Stir in seasonings, including salt and pepper to taste.

Tip: Please refer to the *Key to Ingredients, Nutrients, and Vegetarian Terms,* in the Glossary at the end of this book (under *vegan margarine* and *soy creamer*) for some words to the wise about vegan margarine and soy creamer.

Roasted Vegetables with Butternut Squash

Serves 4 to 6
❖ ❖ ❖ ❖ ❖ ❖ ❖ ❖ ❖ ❖ ❖

1 medium butternut squash, peeled and cut into ½-inch chunks

1 sweet potato, peeled and cut into ½-inch cubes

4 medium Yukon Gold potatoes, unpeeled and cut into smaller cubes than the squash

1 medium onion, chopped

½ small head cauliflower, cut into florets

1 red bell pepper, cut into ½-inch slices

2 cloves garlic, minced

¼ cup extra-virgin olive oil

¼ teaspoon sea salt

¼ teaspoon ground pepper

1 teaspoon dried basil

1 teaspoon dried marjoram

Most varieties of winter squash are exceptionally high in beta carotene, iron, calcium, magnesium, and potassium and the butternut squash is no exception. The squash should be obtained as close to harvest as possible, and cooked soon after.

This dish is dedicated to our friend Tom Classen of Fairbanks, Alaska.

Preparation:
In a large, shallow baking dish combine the butternut squash, potatoes, onion, cauliflower, red pepper and garlic. Drizzle the olive oil over the vegetables; then sprinkle with salt, pepper, basil, and marjoram; toss to coat the vegetables.

Bake uncovered at 400 degrees F for about 40 minutes, or until the potatoes and other vegetables are tender.

Tip: You'll know the butternut squash by its buff outer skin, its long neck and bulbous base, which contains the seeds. Avoid those with green outer skins that indicates a harvest before maturity. Usually, the harvest time is November, although some markets offer these squashes year-round.

Miso Gravy

Yields about 1½ cups

❖ ❖ ❖ ❖ ❖ ❖ ❖ ❖ ❖ ❖ ❖ ❖

2 teaspoons white miso

¾ cup vegetable both

2 tablespoons minced Vidalia or other onion

1 clove garlic, minced

2 ½ tablespoons flour

½ cup soy milk, unflavored

1 teaspoon dried thyme

2 tablespoons olive oil

½ teaspoon tamari

Sea salt

Ground pepper

A fine gravy makes a meal more sensuous. Serve this one over Mashed Yukon Potatoes, steamed cauliflower, grain-based dishes, nut roasts, or veggieburgers.

Preparation:
Place the miso and a half-cup of the vegetable broth in a small bowl and whisk until blended. Set aside.

Over medium heat, sauté minced onion and garlic in olive oil for 4 or more minutes, until onion is slightly browned. Add flour and stir. Then add the remaining ¼ cup vegetable broth and soy milk; whisk into pot, stirring as mixture thickens. Bring to a boil. Add thyme, tamari and miso mixture, cooking for an additional minutes. Add salt and pepper to taste.

Tip: We recommend "mellow white miso" listed under miso in the *Key to Ingredients, Nutrients, and Vegetarian Terms* in our Glossary.

Apple Sauce Sweetened with Agave Nectar

Serves 6 to 8

❖❖❖❖❖❖❖❖❖❖❖❖❖❖

3 pounds of apples (combined green and MacIntosh)

½ cup apple juice or cider

1½ tablespoons fresh lemon juice

1 large cinnamon stick

6 tablespoons agave nectar

½ teaspoon powdered ginger

Agave nectar comes from the inside of a cactus-like plant. It's the perfect substitute for honey in any recipe. The plant's flowering date plays a significant role in the lives of bats along the southern U.S. border, and the bats in turn pollinate the plant. Cattle ranching is its biggest threat.

Preparation:

On cutting board, peel, core and slice the apples into quarters, and then into quarters again. Place the apple pieces in a medium pot with apple juice or cider, lemon juice and the cinnamon stick. Bring to boil over medium heat, and then lower heat to medium-low, stirring occasionally and cooking for 15 to 20 minutes, until apples have fallen apart. Then add agave nectar and ginger. Mash lightly. Serve apple sauce warm or cold.

Breads, Muffins and Accompaniments

Bananas, pumpkins, dates, nuts, berries, and the smell of bread just out of the oven. Open a bakery in your kitchen, and make the perfect bread for your table or a festive gift.

Banana Almond Bread

Pumpkin Bread with Dates and Pecans

Cranberry Nut Bread

Sweet Corn Bread

Sourdough Fruit Muffins

Sour Cream Coffee Cake

Banana Almond Bread

Serves about 8

❖ ❖ ❖ ❖ ❖ ❖ ❖ ❖ ❖ ❖ ❖

¼ cup vegan margarine

2 large bananas

1 cup Florida Crystals natural sugar

Ener-G Egg Replacer (mix according to box instructions to make equivalent of 2 eggs)

2 cups sifted, unbleached white flour

¼ teaspoon salt

1 teaspoon baking powder

1 teaspoon baking soda

¼ cup sliced or slivered almonds or ½ cups blueberries – or both

1 teaspoon almond extract

Making this bread is one of the most healthful projects young people can enjoy at home or at school. Let young chefs know that the best way to ensure the well-being of banana growers and the environment is to choose organic bananas.

Preparation:

Cream soy margarine and sugar in a bowl. Mash bananas on piece of waxed paper. Add egg replacer blend with margarine and sugar in same bowl. Mix all together and add bananas. Sift flour with baking powder, soda, and salt. Add almond extract with chopped nuts or blueberries to mixture. Bake at 325 degrees to 350 degrees F in a greased 9-by-5-by-2½ -inch metal bread pan for 1 hour or until a toothpick inserted in the center comes out clean. Let cool in the pan on a rack for 10 minutes before unmolding to finish cooling on the rack. Slice after completely cool.

Tip: The bread pan must be metal for best results. Please refer to the *Key to Ingredients, Nutrients, and Vegetarian Terms,* in the Glossary at the end of this book (under *vegan margarine, Egg Replacers, Florida Crystals* natural sugar, and *baking powder*) for some words to the wise about those ingredients.

Pumpkin Bread with Dates and Pecans

Makes 4 one-pound loaves

❖ ❖ ❖ ❖ ❖ ❖ ❖ ❖ ❖ ❖ ❖

4 cups Florida Crystals natural sugar

One 29-ounce can of pumpkin

Ener-G Egg Replacer (mix according to box instructions to make equivalent of 3 eggs)

1 cup canola or vegetable oil

5 cups all-purpose flour

1 teaspoon baking soda

2 teaspoons cinnamon

1½ teaspoons ground cloves

1 teaspoon salt

2 cups coarsely chopped dates

2 cups walnuts or pecans, coarsely chopped

Delicious and moist, Pumpkin Bread with Dates and Pecans is a creative variation on the Thanksgiving theme. This recipe will result in four one-pound loaves; they usually disappear quickly. Extra loaves can be frozen for later, or, better yet, shared.

Preparation:

Heat oven to 350 degrees F. Grease four 9-by-5-by-2½ -inch loaf pans. Combine sugar, pumpkin and egg replacer blend in large bowl, and beat by hand or with mixer until well blended. Add the oil, and beat to combine. Thoroughly blend in the flour, soda, cinnamon, cloves, and salt. Stir in the dates and nuts. Fill prepared pans three-fourths full to allow for rising during baking.

Bake about 1 hour or until a toothpick, inserted mid-loaf, comes out clean and the bread has pulled away slightly from sides of pan. Cool before slicing.

Tip: Highest in mono-unsaturates and lowest in saturated fat, canola is a good choice for when you need to use oil for cooking. Find information about *Florida Crystals* natural sugar and *egg replacers* in the Glossary's the *Key to Ingredients, Nutrients, and Vegetarian Terms.*

Cranberry Nut Bread

Makes 1 loaf

❖ ❖ ❖ ❖ ❖ ❖ ❖ ❖ ❖ ❖ ❖

2 cups flour

1 teaspoon salt

1½ teaspoons baking powder

½ teaspoon baking soda

1 cup Florida Crystals natural sugar

Rind of ½ orange, grated

Juice of 1 orange mixed with water to measure ¾ cup of liquid

Ener-G Egg Replacer (mix according to box instructions to make equivalent of 1 egg)

1 tablespoon soy margarine

1 cup halved cranberries, frozen or fresh

½ cup pecans or walnuts, chopped

Cranberries are a holiday tradition, and this bread shows them in an exciting new light. Cranberry Nut Bread is rich and moist, with a blend of sweetness and tartness.

Preparation:

Sift the first 5 ingredients together into bowl. Add rind, juice, and water mixture and egg replacer blend. Stir until partially mixed. Then stir in the melted margarine, cranberries and nuts; mix thoroughly. Place the mixture in a greased 9-by-5-by-2½ -inch loaf pan; let stand until it begins to rise (20 to 30 minutes). Bake at 350 degrees F for 1 hour. Cool before slicing.

Tip: You might wish to try this bread with vegan cream cheese (such as the *Tofutti* brand's "Better than Cream Cheese"). Please refer to the *Key to Ingredients, Nutrients, and Vegetarian Terms*, in the Glossary at the end of this book (under *vegan margarine, egg replacers, Florida Crystals* natural sugar, and *Tofutti,* and *baking powder*) for some words to the wise about those ingredients.

Sweet Corn Bread

Serves 4–6

❖ ❖ ❖ ❖ ❖ ❖ ❖ ❖ ❖ ❖ ❖

¼ cup (½ stick) vegan margarine

⅓ cup Florida Crystals natural sugar

Ener-G Egg Replacer (mix according to box instructions to make equivalent of 2 eggs)

1 cup water

1 cup cornmeal

1 cup all-purpose flour

1¼ teaspoons baking powder

1 teaspoon salt

This is the most authentic of North American delights. Recipes for corn bread derive from Native American traditions. Corn bread fresh from the oven is a perfect companion for *Vegetarian Chili.*

Preparation:

Heat oven to 400 degrees F. Grease a 6-by-9-inch baking dish. Cream margarine, sugar, and egg replacer blend in medium mixing bowl. Add water, cornmeal, flour, baking powder and salt. Pour the mixture into the prepared baking dish. Bake for about 20 to 25 minutes, until top is golden and until tester comes out clean. Serve warm.

Tip: Please refer to the *Key to Ingredients, Nutrients, and Vegetarian Terms,* in the Glossary at the end of this book (under *vegan margarine, egg replacers,* and *baking powder*) for some words to the wise about those ingredients.

Sourdough Fruit Muffins

Makes 12 muffins

❖ ❖ ❖ ❖ ❖ ❖ ❖ ❖ ❖ ❖ ❖

2 cups flour

2 teaspoons baking powder

1 teaspoon salt

1 cup Florida Crystals natural sugar

¾ cup soy milk

½ cup Tofutti brand Imitation Sour Cream

¼ cup canola oil

Ener-G Egg Replacer (mix according to box instructions to make equivalent of 1 egg)

1 cup chopped fruit (apples, peaches, blueberries, or pears)

Sourdough breads are known the world over as a California attraction, and yet the Egyptians record the use of sourdough yeasts 6,000 years ago. These vegan muffins show just how versatile the concept of sourdough can be. They are wonderful for breakfast or any time, served plain or with margarine.

Preparation:

Set oven to 400 degrees F. Grease muffin tins. In one bowl, mix the dry ingredients. In another bowl, mix the wet ingredients. Then add wet to the dry and stir in fruit, taking care not to over-mix the batter. Bake the muffins for 20 minutes.

Tip: Please refer to the *Key to Ingredients, Nutrients, and Vegetarian Terms*, in the Glossary at the end of this book, to find out about the listed ingredients.

Sour Cream Coffee Cake

Serves 8 to 10

❖❖❖❖❖❖❖❖❖❖❖

½ cup vegan margarine, softened slightly

1 cup Florida Crystals natural sugar

Ener-G Egg Replacer (mix according to box instructions to make equivalent of 2 eggs)

1 cup Tofutti brand Imitation Sour Cream

2 cups flour

1 teaspoon Rumford baking powder

1 teaspoon baking soda

1 pinch salt

1 teaspoon vanilla extract

½ cup chopped pecans

1 teaspoon cinnamon

¼ cup packed Hain brown sugar

1 diced apple

Any thoughts that vegan baking won't hold up to tradition are dispelled forever with a taste of this coffee cake. Apple and cinnamon give this cake warmth; sour cream lends a smooth consistency.

Preparation:
Cream the margarine and Florida Crystals natural sugar together; add the egg replacer blend and the vanilla. Sift the remaining dry ingredients together and add them to the margarine mixture alternately with the imitation sour cream. Pour half of the batter into greased and floured tube pan. Combine the chopped nuts, cinnamon, brown sugar and apple, and sprinkle half of the mix over the first layer of batter in pan. Pour the remaining batter into pan and top it off with the remaining nut mixture. Bake at 350 degrees F for 45 minutes or more, until a toothpick comes out clean.

Tip: Please refer to the *Key to Ingredients, Nutrients, and Vegetarian Terms,* in the Glossary at the end of this book, to find out more about the listed ingredients.

Sandwiches and Spreads

Combine ease of preparation with originality. Here are some ideas for your next party, or a light and casual meal. We've selected recipes that are as enjoyable to eat as they are to make.

The Reubenesque

Eggless Salad Sandwich

Tofu Hummos with Toasted Cumin Seed

Baba Ghanouj

Friends' Dip

Bruschetta

The Reubenesque

Serves 2

4 slices traditional rye bread

One 8-ounce package of tempeh

1 cup of drained and pressed sauerkraut

½ cup Reubenesque dressing (see the following recipe)

Vegan margarine

Olive oil

Reubenesque Dressing

2 teaspoons tomato ketchup

¼ cup vegan mayonnaise (such as Nasoya brand Nayonaise or Follow Your Heart brand Vegenaise)

2 tablespoons pickle relish

Preparation:

Mix ingredients together

Here's a stunning new take on one of the old masters. This version of the quintessential New York deli sandwich features the bold strength of sauerkraut and the satisfying texture of tempeh, which is now easily found in large groceries and health food shops.

Preparation:

Sauté sauerkraut in an oiled pan and set aside.

Lightly spread vegan margarine on the outside of each slice of bread, and dressing on the inside.

Slice tempeh into two halves. Cut each half into layers, making four 2-inch-by-3-inch deli slices. In an oiled frying pan, sauté tempeh until it turns golden brown on each side. Then remove the tempeh from the frying pan and set it aside.

Place two slices of bread, margarine side down, into the frying pan. Put two pieces of tempeh on each slice of bread, layer with sauerkraut and remaining bread.

When bread is golden brown, flip sandwich and grill other side until golden brown.

Remove from pan, open sandwich to top with Reubenesque dressing, and cut into halves.

Tip: Please refer to the *Key to Ingredients, Nutrients, and Vegetarian Terms* or the *Shopping Guide* in the Glossary at the end of this book to find out about *Nayonaise.*

Eggless Salad Sandwich

Serves 2

❖ ❖ ❖ ❖ ❖ ❖ ❖ ❖ ❖ ❖ ❖ ❖

1 package (12.3 ounces) Mori-Nu Silken Extra Firm Tofu

1 tablespoon vegan mayonnaise (such as Vegenaise or Nasoya brand Nayonaise)

¼ teaspoon agave nectar

¼ teaspoon salt

¼ teaspoon turmeric

2 tablespoons pickle relish

2 tablespoons red onion, chopped

3 tablespoons celery, chopped

1 teaspoon prepared mustard

2 teaspoons minced fresh parsley

⅛ teaspoon freshly ground black pepper

This typically North American lunch spread can be enjoyed as a sandwich, or as a topping for toasted bagel halves. Or try some on pita wedges, which can be toasted with a touch of olive oil and garlic if desired.

Preparation:
Drain tofu and pat dry with paper towels. Chop tofu into a bowl. In another bowl, mix vegan mayonnaise, agave nectar, salt and turmeric, and add to tofu. Blend remaining ingredients into the spread, and enjoy with bread.

Tip: Please refer to the *Key to Ingredients, Nutrients, and Vegetarian Terms* or the *Shopping Guide* in the Glossary at the end of this book to find out about *Nayonaise.*

Tofu Hummos with Toasted Cumin Seed

Makes 3 cups

❖ ❖ ❖ ❖ ❖ ❖ ❖ ❖ ❖ ❖ ❖

1 tablespoon cumin seeds

2 cups of drained chickpeas, either home-soaked or canned

12 ounces of soft tofu

3 tablespoons fresh lemon juice

2 tablespoons olive oil

¼ cup chopped parsley, and more as desired for garnish

¼ teaspoon or more of sea salt

Ground pepper

A mild, garlic-free alternative to traditional hummos.

Enjoy it with pita toasts, or as a spread on crusty bread.

Preparation:

In a dry heavy skillet, toast cumin seeds over moderate heat, shaking pan until seeds are a shade darker. Transfer the seeds to a cup.

In food processor, purée chickpeas, drained tofu, the cumin seeds, lemon juice and one tablespoon of the olive oil. When the mix is smooth, stir in the parsley. Add salt and pepper to taste. Place hummos in serving bowl. Drizzle with remaining tablespoon of olive oil and garnish with more chopped parsley.

Baba Ghanouj

Makes about 2 cups

❖ ❖ ❖ ❖ ❖ ❖ ❖ ❖ ❖ ❖ ❖

1 large eggplant

¼ cup tahini (sesame butter)

Juice of 1 plump lemon

1 clove of garlic, pressed (or finely minced)

½ teaspoon sea salt

1½ teaspoons olive oil

One chopped tomato and/or a sprig of fresh parsley

Pinch of black pepper (optional)

Baba Ganouj is the classic Middle Eastern aubergine pâté. Warm from the oven, it's the perfect start to an elegant meal. It also serves as a wholesome treat to take along on a day trip or to serve at a vegetarian cook-out. For a variation that's out of the ordinary, try pumpernickel bread and some fresh watercress to make toast wedges or finger sandwiches with the Baba Ghanouj. Delicious for casual summer get-togethers.

Preparation:

Prick skin of eggplant in several places and roast directly on rack of oven at 400 degrees F for 55 minutes, or until soft throughout. When it has reached that point, a bit of juice will begin to trickle out. (You might wish to put a thin pan under the rack to catch the drops of juice.)

Turn the oven off, leave oven door ajar, and let the eggplant cool on the rack for 15 minutes. Using mitts, remove it from the oven. Carefully remove the stem top with a knife; then cut the eggplant in half. You'll notice that the skin easily separates away from the baked pulp. Spoon all the pulp out of the skin, and mash the pulp in a bowl or a shallow baking dish (any spacious container in which you can easily mash ingredients). Add lemon juice, tahini, garlic, salt, pepper if desired, and one teaspoon olive oil, mashing the mix thoroughly as you go.

To serve, spread the mixture into a shallow bowl and drizzle the remaining half-teaspoon of olive oil over the top. Garnish with chopped tomato or a sprig of fresh parsley, or both. Serve with pita crisps, crostini, or flatbread.

Friends' Dip

Serves 2–3

❖ ❖ ❖ ❖ ❖ ❖ ❖ ❖ ❖ ❖ ❖ ❖

1 pound block of firm tofu

3 tablespoons olive oil

2 generous teaspoons of tamari or soy sauce

Clove of pressed garlic

1½ teaspoons brewer's yeast

½ packet of onion soup mix

½ cup red wine

1 cup water

1 small potato, cooked, peeled and thoroughly mashed (or 1 tablespoon of whole-wheat flour)

¼ teaspoon coarse black pepper

Baguette or bakery roll (look for a simple bread made of flour, water, yeast and salt)

The French Dip originated not in France but in North America. A Los Angeles restaurant owner named Philippe Mathieu claimed the distinction of having created the French Dipped Sandwich in 1918. Making a sandwich for a customer, Mathieu inadvertently dropped a sliced roll into the roasting pan. The customer reportedly bought the sandwich anyway and returned the next day with some friends asking for more dipped sandwiches. Thus came the French Dipped Sandwich, named, perhaps, for Mathieu's French heritage, or perhaps for the French roll Mathieu dropped.[8] Here, we restyle the concept in a vegetarian form, to introduce the Friends' Dip.

Preparation:

Slice the tofu thinly using a cheese-slicer or knife. Place the strips into a large, nonstick frying pan along with the olive oil, which will generously cover the bottom of the pan. Heat at a medium-high setting, flipping the strips occasionally, until they turn golden. (You might wish to have a small paper bag on a platter to rest and drain the golden strips as you add more new strips to the pan.)

After about 35 minutes, when all the strips have turned a rich golden (they will be a bit tough in consistency at this point), put them all into the pan together, turn off the heat, and add a generous teaspoon of tamari or soy sauce. The sizzling liquid will impart a rich brown hue in some areas.

Place the soup mix, garlic, and brewer's yeast into the pan over the strips. Then add the water, wine, and another generous teaspoon of tamari or soy sauce. This makes the delicious gravy for the Friends' Dip. Simmer over low-medium heat for 5 to 10 minutes to allow the tofu strips to absorb some of the essence of the gravy. To thicken the gravy, add the small mashed potato to desired consistency, or add a tablespoon of flour. Experiment with this one to discover your own preferences. Serve hot with a sprinkling of black pepper.

(Continued)

Tip: Serve this sandwich open-faced with a side of fresh spinach (raw or lightly sautéed in vegan margarine). Any extra can be enjoyed straight from the fridge in a regular, closed sandwich the next day.

8 Los Angeles Downtown News, "Restaurant Guide 2004" and information supplied by Philippe's "The Original" Restaurant.

Bruschetta

Serves 2

❖ ❖ ❖ ❖ ❖ ❖ ❖ ❖ ❖ ❖ ❖ ❖

½ loaf Italian bread

One large garlic clove, minced

3 or more tablespoons extra-virgin olive oil

One can cannellini beans, drained

One 14.5 ounce can stewed tomatoes

One 14.5 ounce can diced tomatoes, fire roasted

⅓ cup or more of slivered fresh basil leaves

½ to 1 teaspoon dried oregano

2 tablespoons balsamic vinegar

Sea salt

Fresh ground pepper

Bruschetta (pronounced broos-KETT-ah) is an Italian appetizer or antipasti – the original garlic bread. When served with beans, as here, it is known in Tuscany as *fett'unta con fagioli,* "oiled slice with beans" in Tuscan dialect. But the special combination of tomato and beans here is a distinctly North American touch.

Preparation:
Sauté the garlic and beans in olive oil for 2 minutes. Add stewed tomatoes, diced tomatoes, basil, oregano, and balsamic vinegar. Season with salt and pepper, as desired. Simmer for 10 to 15 minutes. Serve on toasted bread.

The Vegan Confectionery: Sweet Adventure, or Rocky Road?

In the United States, some manufacturers have used bovine bone char for the carbon filter used in the refining stage of table sugar, for brown sugar – which is usually just white cane sugar that is toasted or mixed with molasses – for the beige type popularly but erroneously called "raw"sugar, and even for powdered sugar. The high heat transforms the bones into carbon, indistinguishable from that of wood or coal sources. The carbon is used over and over for several years; bone residue does not become part of the finished product.

Because it has long been impossible to determine whether bones, wood, or coal has been employed in the early stages of sugar production, some vegans believe it is best avoided, or they opt for pure maple syrup. Or they select sugars known to use wood and coal in the refining process, such as Jack Frost (white or brown) and the Hain brand. The latter is easy to find, and we have tested it with excellent results in our recipes.

Turbinado sugar is also not bone-filtered; nor is sugar sold under the "Florida Crystals" trademark, even though it is made from cane. Stevia is also free of the bone ash filtering, and is thought to have nutritional value. If you live in the Midwest, you can get white or brown beet sugar, which does not require charcoal filtering as cane sugar does.

Molasses can be derived by separating the sugar without bone ash filtration. But some products might have molasses in the given ingredients, or even be grown on molasses, as yeast is. What then? Does that put them off-limits to vegans?

As vegan chef Joanne Stepaniak has observed, most foods eventually come in contact with animal products, directly or indirectly. Insects and worms land on or burrow through growing plants, and occasionally end up ground up or packaged with them. Food transport vehicles – like the vehicles carry clothing and common household supplies – have components that contain animal by-products, and run over roads, rails, or runways that displaced animals and destroyed habitat when they were constructed. These vehicles also emit fumes and pollutants and

often inadvertently kill free-living animals.Most plant foods are packed in plastic bags that probably contain animal by-products, or paper bags constructed with animal-based adhesives. So perhaps the most practical approach is the following: If a vegetable or a plant-based food contains no overt animal products or by-products, it is deemed vegan.

Adding to the complexities here, a number of vegan food companies have been absorbed by huge multinationals. Takeovers are constant in this area, so you might wish to learn current identities of various products' parent companies if you have a spectrum of products available to you. We also urge support for vegan organic growers. These are farmers who do not rotate their crops with animal agriculture or its products; and they are careful not to harm the myriad small animals on their lands. Their crops are more expensive, but they will only thrive if the public looks them up and participates in their work or buys their produce.

Delectable and Dairy-Free Desserts
Cooking without eggs is traditional. The use of eggs only became commonplace after household refrigeration was available; thus, many cake recipes in 19th and early 20th century cookbooks – including wedding cakes – did not call for eggs. See more in the *Key to Ingredients, Nutrients, and Vegetarian Terms* in our Glossary, under *Egg Replacer.*

Delectable and Dairy-Free
Desserts ❖ Cakes

Some say that desserts are the trickiest to do well. But we have perfected each of these recipes to make your work entirely worthwhile. "I can't believe it's vegan," your guests will say, but we think they'll soon come to see vegan baking as the gold standard. It doesn't get any better than this.

Summer Blueberry Cake

Fresh Ginger Cake

Apple Sauce Cake

Carrot Bundt Cake

Boiled Spice Cake

Coconut Layer Cake

German Chocolate Cake

Coconut Pecan Frosting

Chocolate Pudding Cake

Sweet Dessert Cream

Liberated Chocolate Cake

Distinguished Chocolate Frosting

Summer Blueberry Cake

Serves 12–15

❖ ❖ ❖ ❖ ❖ ❖ ❖ ❖ ❖ ❖ ❖ ❖

1¼ cups maple syrup

¾ cup vegan margarine

4½ cups flour

1½ tablespoons baking powder

¼ teaspoon salt

2 cups orange juice

½ cup water

2 teaspoons almond extract

1 cup blueberries

1 cup sliced almonds

Orange Glaze:

¾ cup Hain Organic Powdered Sugar

2 tablespoons orange juice

Flavored with blueberries and almonds, this simple cake will bring back memories of youth, when the sun shone down and we picked fresh berries, hands and face turning purple. Bring a ray of summer into your kitchen any time of the year with this timeless treat.

Preparation:
Preheat oven to 350 degrees F. Grease a bundt cake pan with Canola Spray Oil.

Allow margarine to soften to room temperature. Do not melt. Place margarine in bowl and cream. Slowly add maple syrup and beat until light and fluffy. Add almond extract and mix. In separate bowl, combine flour, baking powder, salt; then stir to combine. Alternately add flour mixture, orange juice and water to maple syrup/margarine mixture. Blend well. Fold in blueberries and sliced almonds.

Pour into prepared pan and bake 55–60 minutes, or until a toothpick or cake tester comes out clean. Cool in pan 10 minutes. Remove from pan and place on wire rack. Allow to cool completely before topping with glaze.

To prepare glaze:
Combine powdered sugar and orange juice in a small food processor. Pour onto cake.

Tip: Please refer to the Glossary at the end of this book (under vegan margarine) for some words to the wise about vegan margarine.

Fresh Ginger Cake

Serves 10

❖ ❖ ❖ ❖ ❖ ❖ ❖ ❖ ❖ ❖ ❖

1 cup molasses (mild)

1 cup Florida Crystals natural sugar

1 cup peanut oil

2½ cups flour

1 teaspoon ground cinnamon

½ teaspoon ground cloves

½ teaspoon ground black pepper

2 teaspoons baking soda

4 ounces fresh ginger, peeled, sliced, and finely chopped

Ener-G Egg Replacer (mix according to box instructions to make equivalent of 2 eggs)

Fine parchment paper for baking

We've adapted this spiced treat from David Lebovitz's *Room for Dessert,* and you'll surely want to leave room for it. Blended into this cake's irresistibly moist texture is a touch of real ginger root, to bring a bold and piquant character to your table.

Preparation:

Heat oven to 350 degrees F with rack in the central position. Using a circle of fine parchment paper, line a 9-inch round cake pan with 3-inch sides, or a 9½-inch springform pan.

Mix together the molasses, sugar, and oil. In another bowl, sift together the flour, cinnamon, cloves, and black pepper.

In a small saucepan, bring 1 cup water to a boil. Stir in baking soda, and then mix hot water into molasses mixture. Stir in ginger.

Gradually whisk the dry ingredients into batter. Add the egg replacer blend and continue mixing until everything is thoroughly combined. Pour the batter into prepared cake pan, and bake for about one hour, until the top of the cake springs back lightly when pressed or until a toothpick inserted into center comes out clean. If the top of the cake browns too quickly before the cake is done, drape a piece of foil over it and continue baking.

Cool cake for at least 30 minutes. Run a knife around edge of cake to loosen it from pan. Invert cake onto a cooling rack, and peel off parchment paper.

Tip: Serve dusted with Hain Organic Powdered Sugar.

Apple Sauce Cake

Serves 4–6

❖ ❖ ❖ ❖ ❖ ❖ ❖ ❖ ❖ ❖

½ cup safflower oil

1 cup Florida Crystals natural sugar

2 cups flour

½ teaspoon salt

½ teaspoon cloves

1 teaspoon cinnamon

½ teaspoon nutmeg

1 teaspoon baking soda

1 cup raisins

1 cup hot apple sauce without sugar (To make your own unsweetened apple sauce, use the recipe under *Kind Complements* but omit the agave nectar.)

A handful of chopped walnuts or pecans (optional)

Here's a warm dessert to celebrate the season of the harvest. The aroma evokes a picture of covered bridges, winding roads, and the falling leaves of autumn.

Preparation:
Mix the oil and sugar. Combine the spices and raisins with flour and spoon this into the oil/sugar mix, alternating with hot applesauce. Cream until smooth. Pour into greased and floured 6-by-10-inch pan. Bake at 350 degrees F for 45 minutes.

Tip: Find information about *Florida Crystals* natural sugar in the Glossary's the *Key to Ingredients, Nutrients, and Vegetarian Terms.*

Carrot Bundt Cake

Serves 10–12

❖ ❖ ❖ ❖ ❖ ❖ ❖ ❖ ❖ ❖ ❖

3 cups grated carrots

2 cups Florida Crystals sugar

1¼ cups safflower oil

Ener-G Egg Replacer (mix according to box instructions to make equivalent of 5 eggs)

1 teaspoon vanilla extract

2 cups flour

3 teaspoons baking powder

1 teaspoon baking soda

1 teaspoon salt

2 teaspoons cinnamon

⅔ cup pecans or walnuts, chopped

⅓ cup raisins

Frosting for Carrot Bundt Cake:

½ cup (8 tablespoons) vegan margarine

One 8-ounce package of Tofutti "Better than Cream Cheese"

1 pound Hain Organic Powdered Sugar

½ teaspoon vanilla extract or coconut extract

1 cup shredded coconut

The term "Bundt" describes a ring shaped cake baked in a tube pan that has fluted sides. The word was originally a trademark. Its graceful style transforms the classic carrot cake into a conversation piece.

Preparation:
Mix flour, baking powder, natural sugar, salt, baking soda, and cinnamon together. Add safflower oil and stir well. Add the egg replacer blend and vanilla extract. Mix well. Add the grated carrots. Mix again, stirring in the nuts and raisins.

Pour the batter into a 12-cup oiled and floured Bundt pan. Bake at 350 degrees F for 55 to 60 minutes. Remove from oven and cool on wire rack. To remove the cake from the pan, use a knife to loosen it from the sides of the pan, and then invert it onto a serving plate. Frost the cake after it has cooled completely (see the following recipe), and then refrigerate.

Tip: Find information about *Florida Crystals* natural sugar in the Glossary's the *Key to Ingredients, Nutrients, and Vegetarian Terms.*

Frosting Preparation:
Leave margarine out in room temperature to soften slightly, then combine with the refrigerated package of Tofutti "Better than Cream Cheese." Add 1 pound Hain Organic Powdered Sugar, the vanilla or coconut extract, and 1 cup shredded coconut. Combine in food processor. Stir in shredded coconut.

Tip: Please refer to the Glossary at the end of this book to find out about *Tofutti* vegan products.

Boiled Spice Cake

Serves 8–10

❖ ❖ ❖ ❖ ❖ ❖ ❖ ❖ ❖ ❖ ❖

½ teaspoon ground cloves

1½ cups Florida Crystals natural sugar

1½ cups raisins

¾ teaspoon nutmeg

1½ cups water

1½ teaspoons cinnamon

½ teaspoon sea salt

¾ cup vegan margarine

½ cup chopped pecans

Sift together:

3 cups unbleached white flour

1½ teaspoons baking powder

¾ teaspoon baking soda

Priscilla was nineteen when a relative from her grandmother's generation, born sometime around 1890, arrived with other female family members to pass along treasured recipes to mark Priscilla's arrival in the world of adults. This recipe was handwritten on an index card, signed, and given to Priscilla, who modified the ingredients and preparation slightly, as follows.

Preparation:
Place the first seven ingredients in a large saucepan and boil them all together for about 5 minutes until the raisins puff.

Remove boiled mixture from heat and add ¾ cup vegan margarine. When melted, add sifted flour mixture and ½ cup chopped pecans to mixture. Blend and pour into 12-cup fluted tube bundt pan. The bundt pan should be greased by spraying with canola-oil cooking spray.

Bake at 350 degrees F for about 35 to 45 minutes until cake tester comes out clean.

Tip: Find information about *Florida Crystals* natural sugar, *vegan margarine,* and *cooking spray* in the Glossary's the *Key to Ingredients, Nutrients, and Vegetarian Terms.*

Coconut Layer Cake

Serves 8 to 10

❖ ❖ ❖ ❖ ❖ ❖ ❖ ❖ ❖ ❖ ❖

Batter:

2¾ cups cake flour

1 tablespoon baking powder

½ teaspoon cream of tartar

½ teaspoon salt

½ cup soy margarine

1⅓ cups Florida Crystals natural sugar

Ener-G Egg Replacer (mix according to box instructions to make equivalent of 3 eggs)

2 teaspoons vanilla extract

2 cups unflavored soy milk

Sumptuous and showy, the *Coconut Layer Cake* is a baker's tour de force.

Before you start, you'll need fine parchment paper for baking. This rich cake generously serves 8 to 10 guests.

Preparation:
Heat the oven to 350 degrees F with the baking rack in the central slot. Lightly grease three 8-inch round cake pans and line each pan with a parchment paper circle.

In a mixing bowl, sift together the flour, baking powder, cream of tartar and salt; set the bowl aside.

Cream margarine in another (large) mixing bowl for one minute, using mixer on medium speed. Continue beating, gradually adding sugar, for 3 to 4 minutes, scraping down sides of bowl.

Add the egg replacer blend, the vanilla extract, and ¼ cup of soy milk and beat on the low setting for one minute.

Using a rubber spatula to hand-stir the batter, add the flour mixture and remaining soy milk in separate batches, starting and ending with flour. Beat lightly between the additions until the ingredients are well blended.

Pour the batter, dividing it equally, into prepared pans. Smooth the tops with the rubber spatula.

Bake for 22 to 25 minutes, until the top of the cake springs back when lightly touched at the center. Remove the pans from the oven and cool on rack for 10 minutes. While oven is still hot, toast 1½ cups large-flake dried

(Continued)

Custard Cream Layer:

½ cup Florida Crystals natural sugar

6 tablespoons cake flour

4 tablespoons coconut cream powder

Pinch of salt

2 cups unflavored soy milk

1 teaspoon coconut extract

⅓ cup shredded coconut

White Frosting:

1½ cups large-flake dried coconut

4 cups sifted Hain Organic Powdered Sugar

½ cup soy margarine

½ teaspoon salt

2 teaspoons vanilla extract

6 tablespoons non-dairy creamer

coconut on a baking sheet at 350 degrees F for 7 minutes, or until flakes turn golden. Watch coconut closely because flakes can burn easily. Remove them from the oven to cool.

Slide a thin knife around the cake layers to detach them from the pans. Invert the cake layers and peel away the paper liners. Let the cake layers cool right-side-up on racks for at least 1½ hours.

Meanwhile, to make the Coconut Custard Cream, combine sugar, cake flour, coconut cream powder and salt in a large saucepan. Whisk in ½ cup of soy milk and beat the mixture until it is smooth. Whisk in the remaining soy milk.

Cook over medium-low heat for about 5 minutes, whisking gently but constantly until thickened. Cook for 2 minutes more. Stir in coconut extract and ⅓ cup shredded coconut.

Pour the finished custard into small bowl and smooth the top with the rubber spatula; cover surface with wax paper. Refrigerate until cooled.

To make the White Frosting, place sifted powdered sugar, margarine, salt, vanilla extract and soy creamer in bowl of electric mixer fitted with beaters. Beat for 2 minutes with the mixer set to low speed – to prevent sugar from spilling out of the bowl. Increase speed and beat until smooth and creamy. Add more soy creamer if needed to make frosting spreadable.

To assemble cake, put one layer on serving plate and ice with half the pastry cream. Add second layer and ice with remaining pastry cream. Place third layer on top. Cover sides and top of cake generously with frosting. Sprinkle with toasted coconut, covering the sides and top of the cake.

Tip: Please refer to the Glossary at the end of this book for information about various listed ingredients.

German Chocolate Cake

Serves 8

❖ ❖ ❖ ❖ ❖ ❖ ❖ ❖ ❖ ❖ ❖

3 cups flour

⅔ cup unsweetened cocoa

2 teaspoons baking soda

1¾ cups Florida Crystals natural sugar

1 teaspoon salt

2 cups cold water

½ cup plus 2 tablespoons of canola oil

2 tablespoons fresh lemon juice

1 tablespoon vanilla extract

What North American cookbook would be complete without German Chocolate Cake? It might come as some surprise that the recipe was not brought to the midwestern United States by German immigrants, but created here. In 1852, Sam German introduced German's Sweet Chocolate for Baker's Chocolate Company. It was this "German Chocolate" that was used by bakers to make what we now know as German Chocolate Cake. The first published recipe for German's chocolate cake showed up in a Dallas newspaper in 1957 and quickly gained immense popularity.[9]

Preparation:

Mix the flour, cocoa, baking soda, sweetener, and salt together. Sift them or beat thoroughly with a fork to be sure there are no lumps of baking soda.

In a separate bowl, mix the water, canola oil, lemon juice, and vanilla extract.

Whisk the wet and dry ingredients to blend them into a batter. Pour the batter into two greased and floured 9-inch round cake pans or one 9-by-13-by-2-inch pan. Drop pans with batter several times from 6 inches above counter or floor to bring air bubbles to surface and pop them. Bake at 350 degrees F for 25–30 minutes (until a cake tester comes out dry). After completely cooled, frost with *Coconut Pecan Frosting,* on next page.

Tip: 100% organic, unsweetened cocoa, which is also fair-trade certified, is available from Chocolate Source (see the Shopping Guide in the Glossary).

---

9 Mike Mailway, in a column published in the *Seattle-Post Intelligencer* in March 2004, reported that Sam German was of English descent. An earlier article containing similar details about the history of the cake appeared in the *Wisconsin State Journal* in December of 1997. Although all of the articles name Sam German, not a one that we could find names the "Texas homemaker" who actually created the recipe that the paper published.

Coconut Pecan Frosting

Ingredients

❖ ❖ ❖ ❖ ❖ ❖ ❖ ❖ ❖ ❖ ❖

¾ cup vanilla soy milk

½ cup Florida Crystals natural sugar

7 tablespoons of soy margarine

1 teaspoon coconut extract

Egg replacer (mix 4 teaspoons "Ener-G" egg replacer with 3 tablespoons of water and beat until frothy)

1⅓ cups shredded coconut

1 cup chopped pecans

This irresistible frosting is the classic decorative flourish for the German Chocolate Cake. The use of egg replacer makes it more wholesome than its earlier counterpart – and not the slightest bit more resistible.

Preparation:

Put soy milk, sugar, margarine and coconut extract in a sauce pan. Mix egg replacer and add to pan with rest of ingredients. Cook over low heat, stirring frequently until thickened. Remove from heat and stir in 1⅓ cups coconut and a cup of chopped pecans. Let cool until spreadable.

Spread between the layers and on top, leaving the sides bare.

Chocolate Pudding Cake

Serves 6 to 8

❖ ❖ ❖ ❖ ❖ ❖ ❖ ❖ ❖ ❖ ❖

1¼ cups Florida Crystals natural sugar

1 cup flour

2 teaspoons baking powder

⅛ teaspoon salt

1 ounce unsweetened chocolate

2 tablespoons soy margarine

½ cup soy milk or coconut milk

½ teaspoon vanilla extract

½ cup Hain brown sugar

4 tablespoons unsweetened cocoa

1 cup cold water

This one is exciting to do and the preparation makes quite a show for any onlookers who happen to be in the kitchen. Yes, you do pour the water directly on the top layer of cake batter, and yes, it really works. The proof is in your pudding – a heavenly blend of chocolate hues and textures.

Preparation:

Sift ¾ cup of sugar together with flour, baking powder, and salt. Melt the chocolate and margarine gently using a double-boiler or directly on the burner over warm-low heat, stirring frequently. Add the melted chocolate and margarine to the dry ingredients, to create a batter. Add the soy milk and vanilla to the batter.

Pour the batter into a greased 9-by-9-inch pan, covering the bottom of the pan. Combine the remaining half-cup sugar with brown sugar and cocoa. Sprinkle the sugar and cocoa mix evenly over the top of the batter. Now, pour the water directly on the top layer. Do not mix the water into your cake; it will naturally seep in of its own accord, causing the cake to take on a wonderfully decadent hot fudge texture in areas of the overall moist chocolate cake effect. Bake for 40 minutes at 325 degrees F. Serve hot, topped with *Sweet Dessert Cream* (recipe follows); refrigerate the rest and enjoy it cold, without topping, the next day.

Tip: Please refer to the Glossary at the end of this book for information about the various listed ingredients.

Sweet Dessert Cream

Serves 2 to 4

❖ ❖ ❖ ❖ ❖ ❖ ❖ ❖ ❖ ❖ ❖

1 package (12.3 ounces) Mori-Nu
Silken Firm Tofu

¼ cup maple syrup

½ teaspoon pure vanilla extract

¼ teaspoon salt

¼ cup almond oil or hazelnut oil

Serves 2 to 4, so you might double these ingredients if you happen to be serving Chocolate Pudding Cake to more than four people at once. This simple pleasure was created by Mark Shadle, chef and author of the cookbook *It's Only Natural.*

Preparation:
Mix the ingredients in a blender until they're smooth and creamy.

Liberated Chocolate Cake

Serves 8

❖ ❖ ❖ ❖ ❖ ❖ ❖ ❖ ❖ ❖ ❖

1½ cups unbleached white flour

1 cup plus 2 tablespoons natural sugar

6 tablespoons unsweetened nonalkalized cocoa powder

1 teaspoon baking soda

⅛ teaspoon salt

1 cup brewed coffee, cooled

¼ cup canola oil

1 tablespoon white vinegar

1½ teaspoons vanilla extract

½ teaspoon almond extract, or 2 teaspoons chocolate extract

At last, freedom! Here is the classic chocolate cake everybody asks for, and it's now 100% dairy free.

Preparation:

Heat oven to 350 degrees F. Grease and flour one 8-by-8-inch pan. In a large bowl, sift together the flour, sugar, cocoa, baking soda, and salt.

Combine coffee, oil, vinegar, vanilla and almond extract. Stir the two mixes together to make a smooth batter. Scrape the batter into the pan and spread evenly. Bake for 25 to 30 minutes, until a cake tester or a toothpick inserted into the center comes out clean. Cool the cake in the pan on a rack for 10 minutes. Slide a slim knife around the cake to detach it from the pan. Invert the cake and let cool right side up on the rack. Serve plain, dusted with Hain Organic Powdered Sugar, or use our *Distinguished Chocolate Frosting* (recipe follows).

Tip: Star Kay White's Pure Chocolate Extract adds a rich chocolate flavor.

Distinguished Chocolate Frosting

Ingredients

❖ ❖ ❖ ❖ ❖ ❖ ❖ ❖ ❖ ❖ ❖

4 squares (4 ounces) unsweetened bar baking chocolate

2 tablespoons melted vegan margarine

½ cup water

1 teaspoon vanilla extract

Dash of salt

1 pound Hain Organic Powdered Sugar

An eminent finish for the Liberated Chocolate Cake.

Preparation:
Melt the baking chocolate; let it cool slightly and add melted margarine, water, vanilla and salt. Stir in powdered sugar. Spread on cake while frosting is warm.

Tip: Please refer to the Glossary at the end of this book (under *vegan margarine*) for some words to the wise about vegan margarine.

Delectable and Dairy-Free Desserts ❖ Pies and Cheesecakes

These pies are the classics...and we couldn't leave out cheesecakes. Living in a region known for good cheesecakes makes for an exciting vegan challenge. We think you'll find that the bar has just been raised.

Key Lime Pie

Fresh Blueberry Pie

Fresh Strawberry Pie

Spiced Pumpkin Cheesecake

Chocolate Marble Cheesecake

Raspberry Cheesecake

Key Lime Pie

Serves 6–8

❖ ❖ ❖ ❖ ❖ ❖ ❖ ❖ ❖ ❖ ❖ ❖

1 package (12.3 ounces) Mori-Nu Silken Lite Firm Tofu

8 ounces Tofutti "Better than Cream Cheese"

½ cup fresh lime juice

2 teaspoons grated lime or lemon rind

2 packages Mori-Nu Mates Vanilla Pudding Mix

1 tablespoon agave nectar

One 9-inch Arrowhead Mills brand graham cracker pie shell

Key Lime Pie is a lime custard named after Key West, a Floridian seaport. In the South Florida heat, a custard pie without the necessity of cooking found lasting popularity. The sour juice of the Key lime was enough to curdle the condensed milk and egg yolks. Most restaurants now bake it at 160 degrees F because of the worry of salmonella in eggs. No worries about that here, in our egg-free version.

Preparation:
Drain excess water from tofu. Blend Mori-Nu Silken Lite Firm Tofu with fresh lime juice in a food processor until completely creamy and smooth. Add the rest of the ingredients; blend again into a custard. Pour the custard into the pie shell and chill it for 3 or more hours.

Tip: Please refer to the Glossary at the end of this book to find out about *Tofutti* vegan products and *Arrowhead Mills.*

Fresh Blueberry Pie

Serves 6–8

❖ ❖ ❖ ❖ ❖ ❖ ❖ ❖ ❖ ❖ ❖ ❖

¼ cup cold water

5 tablespoons flour

One quart of fresh blueberries

Pinch of salt

1 cup Florida Crystals natural sugar

½ cup water

9-inch baked pie shell

The white blooms of late spring set the scene for the mid- to late-summer crop of delicious blueberries, a native North American plant. Remember those days, when our hands and faces were purple from eating berries right from the garden? Bursting with juicy freshness, this pie celebrates one of nature's most delightful gifts. It's the perfect accompaniment to good conversation and a long sunset.

Preparation:
Make a smooth paste of the ¼ cup cold water, flour and salt. Bring the sugar, ½ cup water, and one cup of the berries to a boil; then add the flour paste, stirring it until it thickens. Remove from heat. When cooled, add the remaining blueberries and stir until they are nicely mixed. Pour the fruit mix into the pie shell. Refrigerate for a few hours or overnight.

Tip: See the Glossary for information about *Florida Crystals* natural sugar.

Fresh Strawberry Pie

Makes one 9-inch pie

4 cups strawberries

1¼ cups juice, such as apple-strawberry or apple-cranberry juice

1 tablespoon agar powder

Pinch of sea salt

1 tablespoon arrowroot

1½ teaspoons almond extract

Fresh mint leaves for garnish

Sweet Dessert Cream (page 126) for garnish

One 9-inch Arrowhead Mills Graham Cracker Pie Crust

Fresh Strawberry Pie brightens any summer table, and the wholesome, natural style of this version brings a well-known pie into its best light. Fresh mint adds a jaunty touch.

Preparation:
Wash and slice the strawberries, and arrange them in the graham cracker pie crust.

Combine 1 cup of the juice, agar, and salt in a saucepan. Bring to boil, reduce heat, and simmer over low heat, stirring constantly for about 5 minutes, until the agar is dissolved.

Dissolve the arrowroot in the remaining ¼ cup juice. Add to the agar-juice mixture, and simmer, stirring for about 4 minutes over low heat, until the mixture begins to thicken.

Remove the juice mixture from the heat and stir in the almond extract. Allow the mixture to cool for 10 minutes.

Pour the juice mixture evenly over the strawberries. Chill in the refrigerator for 2½ hours, or until the mixture sets. Garnish with *Sweet Dessert Cream* and mint leaves, or serve alongside frozen vanilla soy ice cream.

Tip: Please refer to the Glossary at the end of this book to find out about *Arrowhead Mills.*

Spiced Pumpkin Cheesecake

Serves 8 to 10

❖ ❖ ❖ ❖ ❖ ❖ ❖ ❖ ❖ ❖ ❖

1½ cups of graham cracker crumbs

1 tablespoon canola oil

4 tablespoons maple syrup

1 package Mori-Nu Lite Firm Tofu, puréed

8 ounces Tofutti "Better than Cream Cheese"

1 cup canned pumpkin

1 cup Florida Crystals natural sugar

3 tablespoons flour

1½ teaspoons ground cinnamon

½ teaspoon powdered ginger

½ teaspoon ground nutmeg

2 tablespoons pure molasses (mild)

⅛ teaspoon salt

¼ teaspoon baking soda

For a change from pumpkin pie, treat your guests to Spiced Pumpkin Cheesecake. It's a cool variation on a traditional theme, introduced by Akasha Richmond in *The Art of Tofu,* copyrighted by Morinaga Publications. Bookmark this recipe. Your guests are likely to ask for it again next year.

Preparation:
Position a rack at the central height level in the oven, and heat to 350 degrees F. Coat a 9-inch or 10-inch round springform pan with canola-oil cooking spray. Mix graham cracker crumbs, canola oil, and maple syrup together, and press the mix into the prepared pan. Purée the remaining ingredients in a food processor and pour into the crust. Bake for 50 minutes. Let cool for 30 minutes; then refrigerate 5 to 6 hours or overnight before serving.

Tip: See *cooking spray* and *Tofutti* in the Glossary at the end of this book to find out more about these products.

Chocolate Marble Cheesecake

Serves 8 to 10

❖ ❖ ❖ ❖ ❖ ❖ ❖ ❖ ❖ ❖ ❖

9-inch Arrowhead Mills brand Chocolate Cookie Crust

12 ounces softened Tofutti "Better than Cream Cheese"

½ cup Florida Crystals natural sugar

1 teaspoon grated lemon rind

Ener-G Egg Replacer (mix according to box instructions to make equivalent of 2 eggs)

1 cup Tofutti brand Imitation Sour Cream

4 ounces vegan semi-sweet or sweet dark chocolate, melted

The northeastern United States is famous for cheesecakes. Surprisingly, a chef need not use actual cheese to make one. The connoisseur who samples this exquisite dessert will agree: It's a triumph.

Preparation:
Combine tofu cream cheese, sugar and lemon rind; beat until well blended. Beat in the egg replacer blend with the non-dairy sour cream until smooth. Pour the mix into the crust.

Melt chocolate in a pan over hot water. Cool slightly and stir chocolate gently into mixture with a fork until batter has a swirl effect.

Bake at 350 degrees F for 40 minutes, until set. Turn off the heat and leave cheesecake in the oven for another hour, oven door propped open with a wooden spoon. Chill for 6 hours, or overnight.

Tip: Please refer to the Glossary at the end of this book to find out about *Tofutti* vegan products and *Arrowhead Mills.*

Raspberry Cheesecake

Serves 16

❖❖❖❖❖❖❖❖❖❖❖❖❖

Crust:

½ cup maple syrup

¼ cup canola oil

1¾ cups whole-wheat flour

½ teaspoon vanilla extract

Raspberry topping:

One 12-ounce package frozen raspberries

If you thought pure vegetarianism meant abstaining from the world's best cheesecakes, think again. Adapted from Lois Dieterly's cookbook *Sinfully Vegan,* this raspberry-topped cheesecake is a showstopper.

Preparation:
Heat oven to 375 degrees F. Coat a 9-inch springform pan with nonstick canola cooking spray.

To make crust:
In a food processor, combine all crust ingredients and mix thoroughly. Press into the bottom of the prepared springform pan. Prick bottom and sides with a fork and bake for 10 minutes. Remove from oven, reduce heat to 350 degrees F, and set crust aside.

To make topping:
Bring first three ingredients to boil in medium saucepan. Dissolve arrowroot in 2 tablespoons of water and add to hot raspberry mixture. Heat just until thickened – do not boil; the mixture will thicken more as it cools. Set the mixture aside.

To make filling:
Combine cream cheese and tofu in food processor and blend until smooth, scraping down sides as necessary. Add sugar and blend until creamy. Blend in flour and coconut extract. Pour half of filling into prepared crust. Spoon a half-cup of raspberry sauce over the filling. Pour the rest of the filling in the pan and swirl it through with a knife, using care not to mix it completely into the filling. Place on the uppermost rack of the oven. Put a shallow pan filled with water on the lower rack of the oven. Bake for 50 minutes.

(Continued)

¼ cup water

⅓ cup Florida Crystals natural sugar

1 tablespoon arrowroot

2 tablespoons water

Filling:

Four 8-ounce containers of Tofutti "Better Than Cream Cheese"

12-ounce (or 12.3-ounce) box firm silken tofu (such as the firm Mori-Nu variety)

1 cup Florida Crystals natural sugar

1 teaspoon coconut extract

⅓ cup unbleached white flour

After 50 minutes, turn the oven off. Remove the cheesecake from the oven, and carefully spread raspberry topping on top. Return the cheesecake to the oven, and allow it to remain there for an additional hour.

Remove it from the oven and cool it on the counter for 1 hour. Then refrigerate at least 8 hours or overnight before serving.

Tip: See *cooking spray, Florida Crystals* natural sugar, and *Tofutti* in the Glossary at the end of this book to find out more about these products.

Delectable and Dairy-Free Desserts ❖ Festive Treats

Many of these have been passed down in Priscilla's family through generations. Here they are in dairy-free form. We invite you to enjoy them along with us. Make some extra batches for wonderful homemade gifts.

Vegan Cookie Dough

Thumbprint Cookies

Snowy Almond Crescents

Martha Stoddard's Ginger Cookies

Oatmeal Coconut Chocolate Chip Cookies

Chocolate Chip Brownies

Blackberry-Raspberry Flummery

Apple Cinnamon Crisp

Vegan Cookie Dough

Makes 16 dozen

❖ ❖ ❖ ❖ ❖ ❖ ❖ ❖ ❖ ❖ ❖

1 pound vegan margarine, softened slightly

1⅓ cups Florida Crystals natural sugar

1 teaspoon salt

Ener-G Egg Replacer (mix according to box instructions to make equivalent of 3 eggs)

2 teaspoons vanilla extract

4¾ cups unbleached flour

This recipe provides dough to make the next two traditional holiday recipes – enough for 16 dozen. If you decide to make just one batch of cookies, freeze the unused half of the dough for a future time; or go ahead and make extras so you'll have plenty of homemade gifts.

Preparation:
Use a heavy-duty electric mixer fitted with a paddle attachment.

In a large bowl, cream together the margarine, sugar and salt. Add the egg replacer blend and vanilla, and beat until smooth. Add the flour gradually, beating on low speed until thoroughly mixed.

Tip: See the Glossary for information about the listed ingredients.

Thumbprint Cookies

Makes about 5 dozen

❖ ❖ ❖ ❖ ❖ ❖ ❖ ❖ ❖ ❖ ❖

½ recipe vegan cookie dough on page 138

Vegan chocolate chips

¾ cup strawberry or raspberry jam

These delightful little buttons of jam will grace your table with a traditional holiday atmosphere. "Mmm; what is that?" you'll hear, as the chocolate drops momentarily surprise your guests.

Preparation:
Heat the oven to 350 degrees F. Roll the dough into 1-inch balls, and arrange them 1 inch apart on ungreased baking sheets. Using your finger, indent the center of each ball of dough. Drop a chocolate chip in the center and fill with about ¼ teaspoon of jam.

Bake the cookies for 14 to 16 minutes, or until the edges are pale golden. Let the cookies cool on the sheets for 2 minutes before transferring them to wire racks to cool completely.

Tip: To find vegan chocolate chips, see Tropical Source in the Glossary.

Snowy Almond Crescents

Makes about 6 dozen

❖ ❖ ❖ ❖ ❖ ❖ ❖ ❖ ❖ ❖ ❖

1⅔ cups almonds

½ cup Florida Crystals natural sugar

¼ teaspoon salt

½ recipe vegan cookie dough on page 138

1½ teaspoons almond extract

Approximately 3 cups sifted Hain Organic Powdered Sugar

Here are the classic holiday charmers for your table. Along with other treats in this section, they also make a nice gift idea, arranged in decorative tins.

Preparation:

Heat the oven to 350 degrees F. In a food processor, process the almonds, sugar, and salt until finely ground. In a large bowl, beat together the almond mixture, dough, and extract with an electric mixer on medium speed until the mixture is thoroughly combined.

Roll into 3-inch-long ropes and form crescent shapes. Arrange them about three-fourths of an inch apart on ungreased baking sheets. Bake the cookies for 12 to 14 minutes, or until pale golden, and cool for 5 minutes on the sheets.

Place some sifted confectioners' sugar onto a large tray. Transfer the slightly warm crescents to the tray and sift more sugar on top. When cookies are cool, transfer them to storage tin, shaking off the excess sugar.

Tip: See the Glossary for information about the listed ingredients.

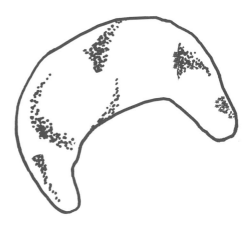

Martha Stoddard's Ginger Cookies

Makes 3–4 dozen

❖ ❖ ❖ ❖ ❖ ❖ ❖ ❖ ❖ ❖ ❖

1 cup pure molasses

½ cup Florida Crystals natural sugar natural sugar

⅔ cup soy margarine

3 tablespoons strong coffee

1 teaspoon baking soda

Ener-G Egg Replacer (mix according to box instructions to make equivalent of 1 egg)

1½ tablespoons freshly grated ginger

Scant ½ teaspoon cinnamon

Scant ½ teaspoon cloves

About 2½ cups unbleached flour

This recipe is a rare gift. As it was handed down through the generations, a new touch was added by each chef, just like a legend whose tellers add flourishes through the years.

Preparation:
Cream the margarine, sugar and molasses; then add the coffee, baking soda, the egg replacer blend, the grated ginger, cinnamon, cloves and flour. Briefly refrigerate the dough.

Place flattened tablespoonfuls of dough onto a lightly greased baking sheet. Bake at 375 degrees F for about 12 minutes.

Tip: See the Glossary for information about the listed ingredients.

Oatmeal Coconut Chocolate Chip Cookies

Makes 4½ dozen

❖ ❖ ❖ ❖ ❖ ❖ ❖ ❖ ❖ ❖ ❖ ❖

2 sticks (1 cup total) softened vegan margarine

1¼ cups Hain brown sugar

½ cup Florida Crystals natural sugar

Ener-G Egg Replacer (mix according to box instructions to make equivalent of 2 eggs)

2 tablespoons vanilla soy milk

2 teaspoons vanilla extract

1¾ cups unbleached flour

1 teaspoon baking soda

½ teaspoon salt

2½ cups rolled oats

1 cup unsweetened, shredded coconut

1 cup vegan semi-sweet chocolate chips

Organic rolled oats lend a hearty texture to this portable dessert. The trick is to let them cool before they begin to disappear...

Preparation:
Heat oven to 375 degrees F. Beat margarine and sugars until creamy. Add egg replacers, soy milk and vanilla extract and beat well. Add flour, baking soda and salt. Mix well. Blend in oatmeal, coconut and chocolate chips.

Drop by rounded tablespoon onto an ungreased baking sheet. Bake for 10 to 12 minutes. Cool for 1 minute on a baking sheet before removing the batch to a wire rack where the cookies should cool completely.

Tip: See the Glossary for information about the listed ingredients.

Chocolate Chip Brownies

Makes about 16

❖ ❖ ❖ ❖ ❖ ❖ ❖ ❖ ❖ ❖ ❖

2⅓ cups flour

1 cup water

½ cup soy margarine

⅔ cup unsweetened cocoa

2 cups Florida Crystals natural sugar

½ teaspoon salt

1 teaspoon vanilla extract

2½ teaspoons baking powder

½ cup chopped pecans

½ cup vegan semi-sweet chocolate chips

Brownies are a popular treat for special occasions. The glossy exterior of this rich brownie gives a crisp appearance, but the brownies will melt in your mouth. Cool before cutting into brownie squares, then wrap and store the squares in the refrigerator.

"Real" (that is, "dark") chocolate has more anti-oxidants than red wine or green tea, and is the second highest source of magnesium among all foods (only seaweed has more).[10]

In a bowl, blend the following ingredients, stirring with a fork to be sure there are no lumps of baking powder.

Preparation:
Mix ⅓ cup flour with water; cook the mixture while stirring until thick; then cool it completely.

Melt the margarine in a separate sauce pan. Add unsweetened cocoa and stir until smooth. Set aside to cool.

Beat sugar, salt and vanilla into the cooled flour mixture, then add cocoa mixture.

Mix together 2 cups flour and baking powder. Add this to the other combined mixture. Then add pecans and chocolate chips. Spread brownie mixture evenly in an oiled 9-by-13-inch pan and bake at 350 degrees F until the top is glossy and cracked, and a cake tester inserted in the center comes out clean – about 30 to 40 minutes.

10 Fact provided by Chocolate Decadence at www.chocolatedecadence.org.

Blackberry-Raspberry Flummery

Serves 3 to 4

❖ ❖ ❖ ❖ ❖ ❖ ❖ ❖ ❖ ❖ ❖

1 cup blackberries

1 cup raspberries

2 cups water

1 tablespoon fresh lemon juice

3 tablespoons corn starch

¾ cup Florida Crystals natural sugar

Old-time British flummeries were made by cooking oatmeal until smooth and gelatinous; in the 18th century, the dish became a gelatin-thickened, cream – or milk-based dessert, topped with sherry or Madeira. Today the name applies to a sweet, soft pudding made of stewed fruit – usually berries, as in this recipe – thickened with cornstarch. This recipe comes from the teacher who, in the 1960s, taught Priscilla the basics of fine cooking.

Preparation:

Add berries and water together and boil in saucepan, stirring and cooking over medium heat for 5 minutes or until berries are soft. Pour the berries and water through a strainer and reserve the fruit liquid, pressing the juice out of berries with a wooden spoon. Discard the berry pulp.

Mix the cornstarch and sugar together. Add this to the fruit juice; stir constantly, and boil over medium heat for 5 minutes, or until juice is thickened and transparent. Remove the mix from the heat, add lemon juice and pour into glass dishes, or stemmed glassware.

Chill for about 4 hours and garnish with a couple of fresh raspberries, and a mint leaf.

Tip: Find information about Florida Crystals natural sugar in the Glossary's the *Key to Ingredients, Nutrients, and Vegetarian Terms.*

Apple Cinnamon Crisp

Serves 4 to 6

❖ ❖ ❖ ❖ ❖ ❖ ❖ ❖ ❖ ❖ ❖

4 to 6 cups apples, pared and sliced

½ cup water

1 teaspoon cinnamon

½ cup vegan margarine

1 cup flour

1 cup Hain brown sugar

Apples were introduced to the Americas in 1620; today, they are especially prominent in the northwestern United States. Wherever you live, you'll enjoy this dish made of tender, juicy apples with a crunchy brown sugar topping. Depending on the type of apple you obtain, the fruity part of this dessert can range from sour to sweet.

Preparation:
Arrange the apple slices to cover the bottom of a greased 9-by-12-inch pan made of oven-proof glass. Pour a half-cup water over the apple slices, and sprinkle them with one teaspoon of cinnamon. Then, in a separate bowl, crumble a half-cup of margarine along with the flour and brown sugar. Spread this mix over the apple slices. Bake for 45 minutes at 375 degrees F, until apples are tender.

Tip: Please refer to the Glossary at the end of this book (under vegan margarine) for some words to the wise about vegan margarine.

Gluten-free Desserts

Chef Barbara Sitomer's Gone Pie Vegan Bakery in New York is a wholesale and online vegan bakery, with an emphasis on superb wheat-and-gluten-free baking. Abundant thanks to Barbara for contributing the following utterly delicious recipes.

Gluten-free Flour Blend

Vegan Sour Cream

Gluten-free Applesauce Cake

Chocolate Sour Cream Cupcakes

Gluten-free Citrus-Almond Custard Pie

Gluten-free Oatmeal Raisin Cookies

Gluten-free Sesame Peanut Butter Cookies

Gluten-free Flour Blend

Makes 5 cups

❖ ❖ ❖ ❖ ❖ ❖ ❖ ❖ ❖ ❖ ❖

1¼ cups gar-fava flour

2 cups brown rice flour

1 cup potato flour

¾ cup tapioca flour

The main challenge of gluten-free baking is to replace the most commonly used baking flours with gluten-free alternatives that mimic both the flavor and texture of traditional wheat products. Plus, they need to taste good! This blend was developed by Barbara Sitomer, the owner of Gone Pie Vegan Bakery. It's the perfect basic flour blend to use in gluten-free recipes.

Preparation:
Sift together, and store in air-tight container. May be stored in air-tight container in the freezer for up to four months.

Tip: When using gluten-free flours, be sure to pack the cup with flour. Gluten-free flours are much lighter, and to get consistent results always pack the measuring cup.

Vegan Sour Cream

Makes approximately 2 cups

❖ ❖ ❖ ❖ ❖ ❖ ❖ ❖ ❖ ❖

1 package soft (not silken) tofu

2 tablespoons fresh lemon juice

3 tablespoons brown rice vinegar

2 tablespoons brown rice syrup

½ teaspoon sea salt

2 tablespoons coconut oil, melted

1 tablespoon canola oil

¼ teaspoon xanthan gum

This sour cream is used in our Gluten-free Chocolate Sour Cream Cupcakes – but you can use it for anything else that calls for sour cream, too. Will store in a tightly-sealed container in the refrigerator for up to one week.

Preparation:
Purée all ingredients in a food processor until completely smooth and uniform. Transfer to an air-tight container and place in refrigerator. Must be refrigerated for several hours – preferably overnight – before using.

Gluten-free Applesauce Cake

Serves 6–8

❖ ❖ ❖ ❖ ❖ ❖ ❖ ❖ ❖ ❖

Wet:

1¾ cups sweetened applesauce

1 cup vegan sour cream (*see recipe above)

¼ cup canola oil

3 tablespoons coconut oil, melted

¾ cup Florida Crystals sugar

This moist cake, with its delicate blend of spices, makes a perfect dessert.

Preparation:
Preheat oven to 350 degrees F. Lightly grease a 9-by-9-inch Pyrex pan.

In a bowl, combine all wet ingredients and whisk together.

In a separate bowl, sift all dry ingredients.

Mix wet ingredients into dry ingredients – but don't over mix.

¾ cup maple syrup

Dry:

1½ cups gluten-free flour mix (*see recipe on page 147)

½ cup millet flour

¼ cup coconut flour

½ cup sorghum flour

1 tablespoon + ¾ teaspoon baking powder

1½ teaspoons baking soda

⅛ teaspoon sea salt

¾ teaspoon xanthan gum

1 teaspoon cinnamon

¾ teaspoon nutmeg

½ teaspoon ginger

⅛ teaspoon mace

Topping:

6 tablespoons Florida Crystals natural sugar

1 tablespoon gluten-free flour mix (*see recipe on page 147)

¼ teaspoon cinnamon

1 tablespoon coconut oil, melted

Stir together all ingredients. Brush flavored sugar on top of cake.

Place dough in pan, and apply topping.
Bake for 1 hour at 350 degrees F.

After cake is removed from oven, cool completely.

Chocolate Sour Cream Cupcakes

Makes about 16 small cupcakes

❖ ❖ ❖ ❖ ❖ ❖ ❖ ❖ ❖ ❖ ❖

Wet:

1 cup non-dairy milk

1 cup vegan sour cream (*see recipe page 148)

1¾ cup Florida Crystals sugar

½ cup canola oil

2 tablespoons coconut oil, melted

Dry:

¼ cup Gluten-free flour mix (*see recipe page 147)

⅔ cup coconut flour

½ cup buckwheat flour

⅔ cup sorghum flour

⅔ cup cocoa powder

1¼ teaspoon baking soda

1 teaspoon baking powder

¼ teaspoon sea salt

½ teaspoon xanthan gum

1 cup vegan, gluten-free chocolate chips

These cupcakes are rich, moist and irresistible – so be sure to make extras.

Preparation:

In a bowl, combine all wet ingredients with a whisk, and mix thoroughly.

In a separate bowl, sift all dry ingredients together – except chocolate chips.

Preheat oven to 350 degrees F. Lightly oil muffin pans.

Pour wet ingredients into dry. Stir together. When almost completely blended, add in chocolate chips. Be careful not to over-mix.

This batter is thicker and stickier than a typical cupcake batter, but don't worry: when baked, these cupcakes are moist and delicious.

Scoop mix into muffin pans. Bake for 20 minutes at 350 degrees F – until firm to the touch, with a slightly cracked top.

Let cool completely before frosting.

Frost with Distinguished Chocolate Frosting on page 128.

Gluten-free Citrus-Almond Custard Pie

Serves 6–8

❖ ❖ ❖ ❖ ❖ ❖ ❖ ❖ ❖ ❖ ❖ ❖

Crust:
Dry:

½ cup gluten-free oats

¼ cup whole, raw brazil nuts

¼ cup gluten-free flour blend
(*see recipe on page 147)

1 teaspoon sorghum flour

1 tablespoon coconut flour

½ teaspoon arrowroot

Pinch cinnamon

Dash xanthan gum

Wet:

2 tablespoons water

4 tablespoons maple syrup

1 tablespoon coconut oil

Filling:

12 ounces extra firm tofu

1 tablespoon lemon rind

1 tablespoon orange rind

2 tablespoons arrowroot

The custard pie re-defined. A creamy dessert that perfect for every occasion.

Preparation:
Preheat oven to 350 degrees F. Lightly oil 9-inch pie pan.

Put the nuts and all dry ingredients in food processor and process until perfectly smooth. Dough should be oily from the nuts. Be sure to scrape sides of food processor to ensure nuts are completely blended.

Add liquids through the spout of the food processor, and process until just together. Careful not to over process.

With well-floured hands, press dough into 9-inch pie pan. This pie crust does not need to be pre-baked.

Place all ingredients in food processor and process until perfectly smooth. This should take several minutes, and you will need to pause and scrape the sides of the food processor. There should be no lumps or rind present in the mixture.

Pour into pie crust.

Bake for 45 minutes at 350 degrees F. Allow to cool.

Refrigerate overnight before serving.

(Continued)

1 tablespoon vanilla extract

¼ teaspoon almond extract

1 cup maple syrup

¼ cup rice syrup

2 tablespoons smooth almond butter

Gluten-free Oatmeal Raisin Cookies

Makes 3 dozen small coookies

❖ ❖ ❖ ❖ ❖ ❖ ❖ ❖ ❖ ❖ ❖

Wet:

2 tablespoons coconut oil, melted

¼ cup canola oil

¾ cup brown sugar

½ cup brown rice syrup

¼ cup maple syrup

⅓ cup water

1 tablespoon vanilla extract

Dry:

½ cup buckwheat flour

½ cup sorghum flour

¼ cup amaranth flour

These cookies are chewy, hearty and deliciously spiced with hints of nutmeg, cinnamon and ginger.

Although oats are inherently gluten-free, not all companies process them on dedicated equipment. We recommend Bob's Red Mill as a reliable source for gluten-free oats. Or, look for "gluten-free" on the package.

Preparation:
Preheat oven to 350 degrees F.

Mix all wet ingredients together in a bowl.

In a separate bowl, sift the dry ingredients together – except for oats, oat flour, raisins and walnuts. After sifting, add oats and oat flour and stir well to combine.

Pour wet ingredients into dry ingredients and stir well. When nearly blended, fold in walnuts and raisins.

Let the dough sit for ½ hour before baking. This allows the oats to absorb

1 tablespoon coconut flour

¼ teaspoon baking soda

⅛ teaspoon sea salt

½ teaspoon xanthan gum

½ teaspoon cinnamon

¼ teaspoon nutmeg

½ teaspoon ginger

2 cups oats

½ cup oat flour (put oats in food processor and process until oats have a coarse flour texture – at least one minute; it's not possible to over-process)

½ cup raisins

½ cup chopped walnuts

some of the liquid, and the dough will "come together."

Scoop dough and place on baking sheet lined with parchment paper or one that is lightly oiled.

Bake for 12 minutes at 350 degrees F. Allow to cool completely.

Gluten-free Sesame Peanut Butter Cookies

**Makes about
2 dozen cookies**

❖ ❖ ❖ ❖ ❖ ❖ ❖ ❖ ❖ ❖ ❖ ❖ ❖

1 tablespoon coconut oil, melted

⅓ cup brown sugar

½ cup agave nectar

½ cup rice syrup

1 cup peanut butter

¼ cup tahini

1 teaspoon apple cider vinegar

½ cup gluten-free flour mix
(*see recipe on page 147)

½ cup buckwheat flour

⅓ cup sorghum flour

2 tablespoons coconut flour

2 tablespoons sesame seeds

¼ teaspoon baking soda

¼ teaspoon xanthan gum

¼ teaspoon sea salt

½ cup coconut milk

Sesame seeds for dipping

The flavors of coconut, peanut butter and sesame create an unusually scrumptious and chewy cookie.

Preparation:
Preheat oven to 350 degrees F.

In mixer, combine liquids, except coconut milk, nut butters and sugar.

Whip until smooth, light and creamy. Be sure not to over-beat nut butter.

Combine dry ingredients. Add coconut milk. Stir together.

Mix together contents of both bowls evenly, but do not over mix.

Scoop dough and roll in sesame seeds.

Flatten and shape into rounds. They spread a little during baking, but retain the shape you make.

Bake for 12–13 minutes at 350 degrees F. Allow to cool completely before serving.

Beverages

Quench your thirst with a drink that's as wonderful as you are. As vegan chef Susan Wu teaches, treating yourself to good health is at the essence of caring about the health and well-being of others.

Vegetable Passion

Carrot Juice with Ginger

Healthful Harvest

Cantaloupe, Mint and Mango Juice

I Am Wonderful

Hot Cranberry Punch

Ginger Lemonade

Vegetable Passion

Fills a pitcher for 4

❖ ❖ ❖ ❖ ❖ ❖ ❖ ❖ ❖ ❖ ❖ ❖

10 carrots, scrubbed and tops removed

5 celery stalks

6 tomatoes

1 bunch of parsley

4 green onions, including white sections

1 clove of fresh garlic

1 fresh, raw beet, cut into chunks

Juicing increases the availability of carotenoids in carrots. Carotenoids are thought to provide health benefits by decreasing the risk of disease and strengthening the immune system. Here is a juice with a strong character to brighten you day and to help protect your health.

Preparation:
Run all of the ingredients through a juicer. Stir the liquid well in pitcher; chill and serve.

Carrot Juice with Ginger

Serves 2

❖ ❖ ❖ ❖ ❖ ❖ ❖ ❖ ❖ ❖ ❖ ❖

8 carrots, scrubbed and tops removed

8 celery stalks

A piece of fresh, raw ginger (about 1 square inch is enough to give this drink a real kick)

Carrot juice is always popular as a healthful refreshment. This version adds the cooling quality of celery – and a special zing, courtesy of fresh ginger root.

Preparation:
Run all of the ingredients through a juicer. Stir the liquid well in a pitcher; chill if necessary, and serve.

Tip: If you bend the celery stalks back just under the line that divides stalk from leafy area, then pull the leafy area down, you can strip out a significant portion of the strings that run vertically through the stalks. It is not necessary to do so, but it might help your juicer to run more efficiently, as there will then be less strings that the machine will need to break down and run through its filter.

Healthful Harvest

Serves 2

❖ ❖ ❖ ❖ ❖ ❖ ❖ ❖ ❖ ❖ ❖

2 apples

4 to 6 carrots

4 handfuls of wheat grass from your local health food shop or co-op

1 thin slice of fresh ginger (or more)

Wheat grass juice is the nectar of rejuvenation, according to many who swear by it. It offers most of the vitamins and minerals we need, including the elusive B12.

Preparation:
Run all of the ingredients through a juicer. Stir well in pitcher; chill if necessary, and serve.

Cantaloupe, Mint and Mango Juice

Serves 2 to 3

❖ ❖ ❖ ❖ ❖ ❖ ❖ ❖ ❖ ❖ ❖

1 small cantaloupe, chilled

2 handfuls of fresh mint leaves

2 mangoes, halved, seeded and peeled

Here is a juice that's unique and special as your good friends are. This recipe makes just over four cups of delicious juice, enough for a gathering of two or three people.

Preparation:
Seed the cantaloupe and discard the husk. Cut the cantaloupe into four parts for easy jucing. Process cantaloupe, mint and mango through the juice fountain. Serve immediately.

I Am Wonderful

Serves 4 generously

❖ ❖ ❖ ❖ ❖ ❖ ❖ ❖ ❖ ❖ ❖

¼ watermelon

2 lemons

Chopped fresh mint

Appreciating yourself is the foundation for appreciating the beauty and energy of all living beings. This affirmation is the gift of Terces Engelhart, at Café Gratitude of San Francisco, California. So here is a cleansing, refreshing drink that makes the most of the watermelon. The rind holds most of the nutrition, and the seeds contain the enzymes. You will get a lot of juice when you work with the whole watermelon, and this recipe will provide approximately four large glasses.

Preparation:
Take one fourth of an average size watermelon, wash it, and cut it into pieces which will fit into a centrifugal juicer. Press the watermelon pieces, including the rind, into the juicer, and pour them into four glasses.

Cut each of the two lemons in half, which leaves you with four lemon pieces. Hand-squeeze the lemons into the watermelon juice, one piece per glass, without seeds.

Garnish with any finely chopped mint. Spearmint works particularly well.

Tips: Use an average size organic watermelon. While any lemons will work, Meyer lemons are especially suitable. Meyer lemons are small, bright and sweet.

Hot Cranberry Punch

Serves 8

❖ ❖ ❖ ❖ ❖ ❖ ❖ ❖ ❖ ❖ ❖

1 cup apple juice

3 cups cranberry juice

½ cup orange juice

3 tablespoons fresh lemon juice

4 whole cloves

1 cinnamon stick

3 tablespoons natural sugar

1 sliced orange

When friends gather to celebrate winter holidays, warm them with the essence of cranberries, orange, and cinnamon. This festive recipe will fill a punch bowl for a party of eight.

Preparation:
In a two-quart pot, combine juices, spices and sugar. Cover mixture and bring to a boil. Strain into warmed punch bowl and garnish with clove-studded orange slices.

Ginger Lemonade

Serves 4 to 6

❖ ❖ ❖ ❖ ❖ ❖ ❖ ❖ ❖ ❖ ❖ ❖

1½ cups fresh lemon juice (6 to 8 lemons)

1½ cups Florida Crystals natural sugar, or 1 cup agave nectar

1 lemon, thinly sliced

3-inch piece fresh ginger, peeled, thinly sliced and crushed

¾ cup water

4 cups cold sparkling water

Fresh mint sprigs for garnish

Lemon juice gets a ginger sparkle with this unusual preparation. Organic agave nectar is a natural sweetener, low in glucose, and a substitute for sugar and honey. Note that if you substitute agave nectar for sugar, the agave mixture doesn't reach the same consistency as the sugar syrup, but does have a luscious caramel-ginger essence. This refreshing combination was first inspired by a recipe in the *Vegetarian Times* magazine.

Preparation:

In medium saucepan, combine ginger, sweetener and ¾ cup of water. Bring to a boil over high heat, stirring to dissolve sugar. Cook for 5 minutes. Reduce heat to medium, and cook for 5 minutes more, stirring often. Remove from heat, and set aside to cool. When cool, discard ginger.

If using agave, combine ginger, agave nectar, and ¾ cup water in a saucepan. Bring to a boil over high heat, and cook for 5 minutes. Reduce heat to medium, and cook for 10 minutes more, stirring occasionally. Remove from heat, and set aside to cool. When cool, discard ginger, and proceed with the recipe.

Transfer it to a pitcher; stir in the lemon juice and 4 cups of cold sparkling water. Add lemon slices, and refrigerate until well chilled. To serve, fill glasses with ice cubes. Pour in lemonade, and garnish with mint sprigs.

Holidays with Friends

Remember George Monbiot's holiday exception?[11] It rings a bell with many people, even long-time vegans, who find that the real challenge often comes at the holidays, when we get together with family members from all generations. With this cookbook on your counter, you'll find that holiday celebrations offer a chance to share new recipes with family and friends. We have spruced up recipes spanning back to Priscilla's great-grandmother's collection, so some of our recipes carry on family holiday traditions continuing for well over a century. This book contains many "old family secrets" to provide you with the key to bringing a winning dish that everyone can enjoy, or opening your home as the preferred holiday hub for years to come.

Here are sample menus for winning holiday menus for all seasons.

11 See page 4. George Monbiot concludes by recommending veganism generally, but makes an exception for "eating meat only on special occasions like Christmas."

Spring: A Season of Rebirth, Activism, and Asparagus

Carrot Juice with Ginger
Artichoke Spread, served with crackers
Zucchini Soup
Spring Pasta with Carrots, Asparagus, and Pesto
Orange Spinach Salad with Romaine Lettuce
Fresh Ginger Cake

Summer: A Time to Celebrate the Solstice

Start with a refreshing juice, such as I Am Wonderful (Watermelon)
Toast Cups with Cilantro Pesto
Veggiessoise
Grilled Tofu with Mustard Dipping Sauce
Mashed Sweet Potatoes
Sesame Green Bean Salad
Key Lime Pie

Autumn: A Time of Thanksgiving

Carrot Pâté, served with wheat crackers and celery
Pumpkin Bread with Dates and Pecans
Walnut Pear Salad
Tempeh London Broil
Mashed Yukon Potatoes
Spiced Orange Broccoli
Spicy Pumpkin Cheesecake
Ginger Cookies

Merry Winterval!

Cauliflower Soup
Green Salad topped with Green Onion Dressing
Tofu Spinach Lasagne
Green Beans with Almonds
Chocolate Marble Cheesecake
Platter of Almond Crescent and Thumbprint Cookies, served on decorative platters or in tins as gifts.
Hot Cranberry Punch

Kitchen Temperature Conversion Chart

Vegan food can be found anywhere in the world, but depending on the region in which you live, you might use Celsius, Fahrenheit, or gas marks to set your oven. Consult an heirloom cookbook and you're likely to find vague terms (by today's standards—such as slow or moderate. Here is a general guide. It does not comprise exact conversions; also, ovens of different makes and models will vary.

Degrees Fahrenheit	Degrees Celsius	Gas Mark	Description
275	135	1	Slow
300	150	2	Slow
325	160	3	Moderately slow
350	175–180	4	Moderate
375	190	5	Moderately hot
400	205	6	Moderately hot
425	220	7	Hot
450	230	8	Hot
475	245	9	Very hot

Glossary

A. Key to Ingredients, Nutrients, and Vegetarian Terms

Agar: Agar is a translucent, plant-based nutritive sweetener, derived from red algae. Chiefly from eastern Asia, it is also known as Kanten, Agar-Agar, or Agal-Agal (Ceylon Agar). Most types of agar are purchased in powder form. Dissolved in hot (usually boiling) water and cooled, agar becomes gelatinous, and has featured in traditional Japanese desserts popular for many centuries.

Agave nectar: A sweetener with a consistency similar to honey, agave nectar is suitable for tea or for baking, and provides the natural minerals iron, calcium, potassium, and magnesium. It is extracted from the pineapple-shaped core of the agave, a cactus-like, Central American plant. When baking, a general rule is to replace 1 cup sugar with ¾ cup of agave nectar, and reduce traditional recipe liquids (outside of this book) by ⅓ and oven temperature 25 degrees F. Vegans avoid honey because bees, who are sensitive animals, rely on the honey they create as their sole source of nutrition in cold weather and other times when alternative food sources are not available. In the process of honey collection, some bees are likely to be killed or injured. Apiculture entails the buying and selling of bees, genetic selection techniques, and artificial insemination.

Al dente: Cooked only until tender but still giving some resistance to the bite. Pasta cooked al dente is slightly firm, not soggy or starchy.

Antioxidants: Chemicals thought to protect cells against environmental smog and other possible carcinogens. Steaming vegetables rather than boiling them is best for retaining antioxidants. Research in the *Journal of the Science of Food and Agriculture* indicates that steamed broccoli, for example, lost 11% or fewer of its three major antioxidants. Microwaving seems especially harsh on antioxidants: microwaved broccoli lost between 97% and 74% of the three compounds; in contrast, one antioxidant was not removed at all during steaming. Dr. Cristina Garcia-Viguera, from the University of Porto in Portugal, explains that "most of the bioactive compounds are water soluble; during heating they leach in a high percentage to the cooking water, reducing their nutritional benefits in the foodstuff." That's one reason more antioxidants would be lost upon boiling rather than steaming.

Baking powder: Rumsford brand, sold in a red container, works well, and is a safe choice because it does not contain aluminum sulfate (also called aluminum salt). Baking powder stays fresh for about one year.

Blanch: To partially cook by placing the vegetable in cold water, bringing it to a boil, then draining it well and refreshing it in cold water to stop the cooking process.

Bread: See *Ener-G bread; rye bread.*

Brown rice syrup: Brown rice syrup is a naturally processed sweetener, made from sprouted brown rice. It is thick in consistency, and mild in taste.

Bulgur wheat: Golden beige grain with an irregular, cracked shape. Best known as the main ingredient in tabouli, its higher nutritional value makes it a good substitute for rice or cous cous.

Bundt cake: Pronounced: bunt (as in "cut") or boont (as in "took"). A ring-shaped cake baked in a tube pan that has fluted sides. Originally a trademark. Source: *The American Heritage® Dictionary of the English Language* (Fourth Edition, 2000).

Butter substitutes: See *vegan margarine.*

Calcium stearate: Additive sometimes found in sweets; usually derived from the fat of other animals.

Canola oil: Mostly tasteless. Low in saturated fat. 1 tablespoon provides 1.6 grams of linolenic acid.

Casein: See cheese.

Cheese: Vegans avoid cheese and products containing whey (liquid part of animal milk) or caseinates (which contain casein, a protein derived from cow's milk). Although most cheese alternatives state that they do not contain lactose, a dairy-derived sugar, closer reading of the ingredient label reveals that they contain casein. This protein is added to give melted soy cheeses the rubbery texture found in cheese made from the milk of nonhuman animals. As a result, few cheese alternatives on the market are vegan. Daiya and Tofutti are brands that are, as we go to press, vegan. See Tofutti. Vegan-Rella is also, as the name indicates, vegan. Soymage Vegan Grated Topping is the vegan answer to Parmesan cheese currently marketed as we go to press.

Chocolate: Bittersweet (in 3-ounce bar) Pure Dark Chocolate by Chocolate Decadence works well in cheesecake and many other recipes. Chocolate Decadence is vegan-owned and -operated. See <www.chocolatedecadence.com>. Paul Newman's brands offer vegan chocolate for cooking or indulging, avoiding chocolate made by enslaved workers. A investigation, published in 2000 by the British Broadcasting Company (BBC), reported that hundreds of thousands of children have been purchased from their parents in Mali, Burkina Faso, and Togo for a nominal price and then shipped to the Ivory Coast, where they are sold as slaves to cocoa farms. These children work 80 to 100 hours a week, and are often viciously beaten if they try to escape. Given these circumstances, we think you'll agree that the extra money you pay for fair-trade chocolate is reasonable. Newman's Own Organics can be found at grocery chains. For more information on Newman's Own Organics (some of them are vegan).

Green & Blacks Organic Unsweetened Cocoa for baking is fair-trade certified, and available from Chocolate Source at 800.214.4926; or visit <http://www.chocolatesource.com> on the Internet.

Chocolate: Look for *Chocolate Decadence, Tropical Source, Newman's Organics, Equal Exchange, Ithaca Fine Chocolates,* and *Yachana Gourmet* brands.

Chocolate chips: Small chocolate drops. See *Tropical Source.*

Cholesterol: Our cells contain cholesterol, naturally produced by the liver. The body needs no additional cholesterol. When cholesterol and fats move through the body, in clusters called lipoproteins, the "Low-density lipoproteins" (LDLs) leave deposits along the walls of the arteries as they travel to the organs. Eventually this process narrows the arteries and obstructs blood flow. Known as hardening of the arteries, this condition is fairly common; but in advanced cases it can lead to heart disease or strokes. Given that LDLs promote atherosclerosis, they are known as "bad cholesterol." "Good cholesterol," found in "high-density lipoproteins" (HDLs), moves back to the liver where it is cleansed. But most cholesterol is in the form of LDLs, and a high blood cholesterol level means high LDL levels. According to a study published in the *Journal of Chronic Disease* (1978), population groups with cholesterol levels of 150 or less are largely free of atherosclerosis. For cholesterol levels above 150, the risk of heart disease increases.

Saturated fats raise your body's natural cholesterol levels, but added cholesterol is found only in animal products, including shellfish. Basing one's diet on plant foods is the best way to keep saturated fat intake low and to avoid cholesterol. A non-smoking vegan's diet has the lowest risk of heart disease, according to nutritional studies. Research also shows that people who eat small meals frequently throughout the day ("nibblers") have lower cholesterol levels than people who fill up at set meal times ("gorgers"). Additionally, exercise and the use of relaxation techniques such as yoga or meditation help. Combined with a low-fat, pure vegetarian diet, they lower one's cholesterol levels and – according to studies published by Dean Ornish – can even reverse heart disease for many people.

Chop: To cut into coarse chunks of the size typically found in canned soups.

Cocoa powder: See *Shopping Guide,* under *Chocolate Source.*

Coconut: Sun-dried, organic coconut for baking can be ordered from *Nature's First Law* through 1.888. RAW-FOOD (1.888.729.3663). See also *Nature's First Law* in the Shopping Guide.

Coconut cream powder: Chao Thai is a popular brand, found in your Asian market or available by electronic ordering through <http://importfood.com/spct5601.html>.

Coconut Milk Beverage: Non-dairy milk by So delicious™. Other products include Coconut Milk Creamers. <www.sodeliciousdairyfree.com>.

Complementary proteins: See *protein.*

Cooking spray: *Spectrum Naturals* offers an organic, canola-oil cooking spray (skillet spray). At the time of this publication, ordering this product is possible by contacting A Different Daisy 740.820.3146 or, if you prefer e-mail, writing to <differentdaisy.com>.

Dice: To chop finely into tiny cubes.

Egg replacers (Ener-G Egg Replacer): A vegan egg substitute comprised of potato starch, tapioca flour, leavening (non-dairy calcium lactate, calcium carbonate, citric acid), and carbohydrate gum. A 16-ounce box makes the equivalent of 100 eggs. For example, for the equivalent of one egg, mix 1½ teaspoons of egg replacer (Ener-G brand) with 2 tablespoons of water and beat with a fork until frothy.

Another egg substitute is ½ mashed banana; some chefs experiment using avocados.

Why an egg-free cookbook? The intensive egg industry, which began by storing thousands of birds in unused military sheds, is widely considered a model for today's intensive animal agriculture. Some people argue that free-range eggs are acceptable, but most free-range eggs come from birds who are also confined, and are eventually killed; male chicks are often deemed disposable. Moreover, the entire human community cannot afford to have and eat free-range domestic animals. So from a practical standpoint alone, the best idea would be for humanity to design and enjoy a rich variety of plant-based culinary approaches. This is our contribution to that adventure.

Ener-G bread: Wheat-free, gluten-free sliced bread, available at some groceries and many health food shops.

Ergocalciferol: See *Vitamin D.*

Fish(es): See *pesco-vegetarian.*

Flax seed oil: Omega-3 fatty acids can be boosted by a teaspoon of flax seed oil per day.

Like kelp and Brazil nuts, flax seed oil has highly concentrated nutrients; don't overdo them. Stick with the product's suggested amount. See also *linolenic acid; canola oil.*

Florida Crystals natural sugar: There is no animal bone char or any other animal by product used in the manufacturing of Florida Crystals, a sugar produced by the Florida Crystals Corporation of West Palm Beach, Florida. No additives, preservatives, or artificial ingredients are added. Internet ordering is possible, through <http://www.floridacrystals.com/>. The customer service hotline is 877.835.2828.

Fruitarian: One who eats foods that ripen and release naturally, so that harvesting does not kill the plant. A fruitarian will eat apples, but not potatoes.

Gelatin (also gelatine): A protein product, manufactured by partial hydrolysis of collagen found in animal bones, hooves, connective tissues, and skins. When added to recipes, it produces a gel, commonly found in marshmallows, mints and clear sweets, and also in pharmaceutical capsules. A similar product known as agar (or "agar agar') can be obtained from vegetable sources. Most "kosher gelatin" isn't vegetarian, but Emes kosher gelatin is made from carrageenan (seaweed-based). Guar gum is vegan.

Genetically modified organisms ("GMO"); genetic

engineering ("GE"): Although these concepts have been heralded by some politicians as a scientific breakthrough to solve world hunger, the reality is something which we should study closely. Opposition to genetic engineering is not "anti-science" but is a critique of products provided through a specific application of scientific personnel and a decision to allocate resources in a way which is tied to the profits of large companies.

Hain organic sugars: These include powdered and brown sugar preferred by many vegans. No bone ash is used in the refining process. The powdered version contains organic evaporated cane juice and organic cornstarch; the brown version contains organic evaporated cane juice. Widely available throughout North America.

Herbs: When using fresh herbs, you must use more than you would of the dry version. As a rule, plan a 3-to-1 ratio. For example, if a recipe suggests 1 teaspoon dry dill, you can use 1 tablespoon fresh dill. (A tablespoon is three teaspoons.)

Honey: See *agave nectar.*

Iodine: Nutrient provided by iodized salt or kelp (about 15 grams over the course of a year, or two kelp tablets a week, is about right), or even coconut. Good levels of iodine help maintain a healthy thyroid, and promote high energy, clear skin, and healthy cholesterol levels.

Iron: Dark green, leafy vegetables and beans are a better source of iron than hamburger or milk. Blackstrap molasses, tofu, prune juice, bulgur wheat, dried apricots, raisins, cashews, and dried figs are also excellent sources of iron. Iron deficiency rates are no higher in vegetarians than in the general population. According to the American Dietetic Association, the higher vitamin C content of vegetarian diets may improve iron absorption.

Lightlife: The company advertises its products as tested GMO-free to the limits of the current testing capabilities. As this book goes to press, the Chick'n Strips product is "Certified Vegan" (expressly defined as containing no animal ingredients or animal bi-products, using no animal ingredient or bi-product in the manufacturing process, and not being tested on animals). The product contains water, textured soy protein concentrate, natural flavors (from vegetable sources), salt, yeast extract, potassium chloride, chicory fiber (inulin), natural smoke flavor.

Caveat Emtor! Note that the same brand, Lightlife, features bratwursts and hot dogs, called Grill Ready Brats and Grill Ready Dogs, that contain eggs; and the brand's Italian sausage, once vegan, now also contains eggs. Read each package carefully, as we cannot predict what products this brand, now owned by ConAgra, will change in the future.

Linolenic acid: The American Dietetic Association recommends that vegetarians include good sources of linolenic acid in their diets. Good sources include flax seed oil, walnuts, and canola oil.

Liquid Smoke: A barbecue smoke seasoning that can be found in most grocery stores in the same section as tomato ketchup and barbecue sauces. It can be ordered electronically through <http://www.colgin.com>. Made by the Richard E. Colgin Company of Texas, Colgin Natural Liquid Smoke contains water, natural smoke flavor, vinegar, molasses, caramel color and salt. Colgin Natural Liquid Smoke does not contain animal by-products, according to the company fact sheet, which we found at <www.colgin.com/liquidsmokefaqs/> For more information, please phone the Colgin Company at 888.226.5446.

Magnesium: Found in green, leafy vegetables; whole-grain breads, and nuts, magnesium promotes strong bones, a healthy heart and a smoothly functioning nervous system.

Margarine: See *Vegan margarine.*

Marinara sauce: A simple pasta sauce made of crushed tomatoes and olive oil, often with finely chopped onion, minced garlic, basil, oregano.

Mince: To chop finely, nearly into a blend (such as minced garlic).

Miso: A paste, either rich dark brown (with a strong taste) or sandy in hue (known as white miso, with a relatively sweet taste), made from soybeans, barley, rice, or a combination of these. Miso is used in spreads, gravies, or as a soup stock. Miso is normally vegan, although some Japanese brands of miso contain a fish extract. Westbrae Natural offers mellow white miso from cultured white rice, organically grown whole soybeans, water, and sea salt. Please see *Westbrae Natural* in the next section's *Shopping Guide.*

Nama Shoyu: Advertised as "The Champagne of Soy Sauces," Nama Shoyu is a raw, organic, and unpasteurized soy sauce, similar to miso tamari. It is manufactured by Ohsawa, and has become their best-selling product. Note: Nama Shoyu contains wheat. See also *Rawganique.com.*

Nayonaise: A soy-based sandwich spread by tofu company Nasoya. On the Internet, see <www.nasoya.com>.

Nutritional yeast: Adds taste and a texture slightly reminiscent of cheese. Red Star Vegetarian Support Formula provides B-complex vitamins including a naturally fermented, non-animal source of vitamin B-12.

Oil: See *organics; cooking spray.*

Olive oil: A monosaturated oil, pointing to positive health benefits. Quality oilve oil includes Extra Virgin, Cold-pressed.

Organics: Products that support sustainable farming, farm worker health, and ecologically-sound processing methods. An official definition adopted by the National Organic Standards Board in 1995 states: "Organic agriculture is an ecological production management system that promotes and enhances biodiversity, biological cycles and soil biological activity. It is based on minimal use of off-farm inputs and on management practices that restore, maintain and enhance ecological harmony." 60 percent of herbicides, 90 percent of fungicides, and 30 percent of insecticides are considered carcinogenic by the U.S. Environmental Protection Agency. The search for alternatives steers consumers to organic products. Now here's the rub: Animal-derived products are often used as fertilizers. Green fertilizers such as seaweed and clover; some gardeners are exploring the use of such products in a practice known as "veganic" gardening. Although organic production on its own guarantees neither a stable livelihood nor long-term environmental sustainability, it undoubtedly takes an important step in the right direction.

Ovo-lacto vegetarian: Person who eats food from vegetable sources, but the prefix "ovo" signifies one who also eats eggs, and the prefix "lacto" signifies one who ingests animal milk products.

Pareve (parve): A kosher classification; made without animal flesh or milk but can contain eggs or fish derivatives.

Pesco-vegetarian: Person who eats a vegetable-based diet but includes marine animal flesh. The idea that marine animals can be compatible with vegetarianism is probably based on the idea that fish swim freely until they get caught, and they don't feel anything when they do. But now that fishing industries have pillaged the open waters, a substantial portion of marketed marine animals grow up in enclosed ponds, or fish farms. And for many years, scientific reports have indicated that fish are sentient and show the same responses we show when we suffer. For instance, a 2003 article in the journal Nature indicates that fish feel pain when impaled on hooks. Fish constantly depend on the delicate sensitivity of their mouths to find food. The idea that fish are not conscious seems

a throwback to the time of Descartes, the French philosopher who believed that animals feel no pain, and only struggle to escape, yelp, or cry as a mechanical response.

Contrary to some company's claims, fish oil supplements do not lower cholesterol levels in the blood, according to a study published in the *Journal of Lipid Research* by S.M. Grundy and M.A. Denke (1990). A diet including fish is not as beneficial as a pure vegetarian diet.

Protein: Most North Americans ingest significantly higher amounts than necessary. Studies have linked excess protein with osteoporosis, kidney disease, calcium stones in the urinary tract, and some cancers. A varied diet with adequate calories should provide enough protein, according to the American Dietetic Association. The position of Association, relying on research published in the *American Journal of Clinical Nutrition,* is that complementary proteins do not need to be consumed at the same time and that consumption of various sources of amino acids over the course of the day should ensure adequate nitrogen retention and use in healthy persons. Most foods contain protein. (Fats and sugar do not.) Tempeh, lentils, beans, broccoli and tofu are excellent sources.

Purée: To finely blend food to a smooth, lump-free consistency – usually in a food processor.

Raw foods, nutrition facts: If you use the Internet, The Vegan Society has a page on raw foods. See <www.vegansociety.com>. Information in paper form can be obtained from Plant Based Nutrition and Health by Stephen Walsh, published by the Vegan Society, The Vegan Society, Donald Watson House, 21 Hylton St., Hockley, Birmingham, England B186HJ. Telephone: 011.44.1.215.231730. In the Shopping Guide (second part of this Glossary), see *Rawganique.com* and *Nature's First Law.*

Rye bread: Traditional rye breads, made from flour, water, salt, yeast and caraway, are vegan.

Scallion: A scallion is one type of immature onion (commonly called green onion), with an edible white base that has not fully developed into a bulb and green leaves that are long and straight. True scallions – generally identified by straight sides of the base, whereas the others have slightly curved bulbs – have a milder taste than other immature onions. Scallions are available year-round but are at their peak during spring and summer. Look for midsized scallions with crisp, bright green tops and long, firm white bases. Scallions, which keep in the refrigerator for up to 5 days, can be cooked whole as a vegetable much as you would a leek. They can also be chopped and used in salads, soups and many other dishes.

Seasoning: See *tamari; Spike.*

Shitake mushrooms: See *Vitamin D.*

Soy milk: A plant-based milk, usually appearing in original, vanilla, and chocolate varieties. Easy to find in most large groceries and virtually any health food shop. Slightly heavier than rice milk. See also *Stony Mountain Botanicals* in the next section's *Shopping Guide.*

Spike: This seasoning appears in two varieties:

original and salt-free. Here are the ingredients listed in the salt-free variety: Defattted nutrisoy granules, granular toasted onion, nutritional yeast, granular garlic, celery root granules, ground dill, horseradish granules, mustard powder, lemon peels, orange powder, parsley flakes, red bell peppers, green bell peppers, white cate pepper, rose hips powder, summer savory, mushroom powder, safflower, parsley powder, white onion powder, spinach powder, tomato powder, sweet Hungarian paprika, ground celery seed, cayenne pepper, ground turmeric, ground cumin, ground ginger, ground coriander, ground fenugreek, ground cloves, cinnamon powder, plus a delightful herbal bouquet of the best greek oregano, french tarragon, french sweet basil, french marjoram, french rosemary and spanish thyme.

Stevia: Stevia is a trademarked, non-caloric additive derived from a Paraguayan shrub *(Stevia rebaudiana).* Although stevia is highly effective in adding sweetness to foods, it is sold as a dietary supplement. Stevia also appears to have medicinal traits: it may have anti-viral properties, and prevent high blood pressure and diabetes.

Tabouli: You can prepare this on your own, with no cooking necessary, using organic bulgur wheat from the bulk section of your co-op or health food shop. Some regular grocery chains offer it too. Also see *bulgur wheat.*

Tamari: Wheat-free soy sauce alternative.

Tempeh: Made from fermented soybeans, and available mixed with spices or vegetables, tempeh has a rough, grainy texture that works well in sandwiches.

Tofu: This versatile staple, made from the curd of the soybean, has no taste until you mix or marinate it with other ingredients, which it absorbs wonderfully. Comes in a range of textures from soft (good for dips) to extra-firm (good for stir-frying). It is no easy matter to find a non-GMO brand that also has an appealing texture. Usually, one has to sacrifice one quality or the other. But at the time of this writing, the Vitasoy brand offers an excellent packaged, block tofu that is made from non-genetically modified soybeans. (We found it in a Chinese grocery.) Call 1.800.848.2769 for locations near you or look for this brand in the *Shopping Guide* for Internet instructions.

Tofutti: Tofutti Brands, Inc. produces soy-based products for health food shops. The company is based in New Jersey and can be reached at 908.272.2400. All products are free of cholesterol, lactose and dairy derivatives. The lactic acid used by Tofutti is of vegetable origin, not dairy. Makes a sour cream that works well as a substitute for the dairy version. Tofutti's "Better Than Cream Cheese" is one cream cheese substitute that is, as we go to press, vegan; and it works in precisely the same way any traditional cream cheese would work. Also see *cheese.*

Tropical Source: Company using "dedicated" machinery for vegan chocolate (no dairy traces). 10-ounce packages of dark chocolate "semi-sweet chips" sold at grocers with vegetarian products or health food shops. These are small chocolate drops for delicate desserts; they can be found in co-ops and in most groceries with good natural food sections. The company puts effort into informing consumers that chocolate used in their product is purchased only from farms where farmers and workers are treated well.

Vegan (VEE-gun): 1. Pure vegetarian; a recipe using only plant-derived products. 2. A person who has embraced an ethic of concern and respect for sentient life.

Vegan margarine: An example of vegan margarine available at the time of this publication is Shedd's Willow Run Soybean Margarine by Unilever. When looking for vegan margarine, avoid whey and D-3. Margarines will contain some form of vitamin D fortification; vegans choose D-2 (ergocalciferol). This is important to note, because vitamin D-3, a sheep or fish oil derivative, is less expensive than vitamin D-2, so most margarines will contain D-3. See also *Vitamin D.*

Vegenaise: Non-dairy, vegan mayonnaise by Follow Your Heart. <www.followyourheart.com>.

Vitamin B-12: On rare occasions, vitamin B-12 (needed for cell division and blood formation) does present a concern for pure vegetarians, but the problem is easily solved with a vegan dietary supplement or fortified cereal, or 1 to 2 teaspoons of Red Star T-6635+ nutritional yeast. The body stores this vitamin for a long time, so the use of extra amounts carries over. Breast milk is an adequate source for infants only if the mother's intake is adequate. Absorption of vitamin B-12 becomes less efficient as the body matures, so the American Dietetic Association recommends supplements for all older (albeit young at heart) vegetarians.

Vitamin C: A nutrient that is plentiful in the vegan diet, particularly in citrus fruits and dark green vegetables. See also *iron.*

Vitamin D: According the American Dietetic Association, vitamin D is poorly supplied in all diets unless vitamin D- fortified foods are consumed. Citing the *Journal of Nutrition,* the Association recommends sun exposure to hands, arms, and face for 5 to 15 minutes per day in order to absorb sufficient amounts of the nutrient. People with dark skin or those who live at northern latitudes or in cloudy or smoggy areas may need more exposure. Use of sunscreen interferes with vitamin D synthesis. Thus, if your dermatologist recommends sunscreen, or your sun exposure is inadequate, vitamin D supplements are recommended for vegans, especially our vegan elders. In the winter, the body cannot make vitamin D from sunlight and it may be beneficial for bone health to include about 5 micrograms of the vegan form (ergocalciferol, also known as D-2) daily. This can be obtained from about 10 grams of dried shitake mushrooms as well as from supplements. Due to the high rate of bone building taking place, infants should receive a vitamin D supplement in winter. See also *Vegan margarine.*

Whey: An animal product made of the liquid component of milk.

B. Shopping Guide

Vegan ingredients are readily available throughout North America. This section is provided for those who wish to confirm that a product will be suitable to you, and to give you an idea of what can be ordered. Sometimes, recommended companies will change brand names, change the menu of products or the names of their products, or even change the ingredients. So preparing pure vegetarian dishes means focusing carefully on details, and being prepared for the possibility of changing your recipe. But for all good chefs, anticipation, experimentation, and flexibility are part of the art and the adventure. All good chefs learn from others, then adapt the ideas to suit their own style.

A Different Daisy: See *Different Daisy.*

Arrowhead Mills: Arrowhead Mills is now owned by The Hain Celestial Group, one of the largest North American organic food companies. Today Arrowhead Mills still purchases many of its ingredients locally from its original suppliers. Its product line is advertised as "over 87% organic." You may notice that the recommended vegan pie crusts have a Kosher symbol with the word "dairy" under the symbol. This signifies that Kosher laws permit the crusts to be eaten with dairy products – not that they include or processed with dairy products. We have confirmed with the company that the recommended crusts are indeed vegan.

Chocolate Source: Green & Blacks Organic Unsweetened Cocoa for baking is fair-trade certified, 100% organic cocoa, and available from Chocolate Source at 800.214.4926; or visit <http://www.chocolatesource.com> on the Internet.

Different Daisy: Vegan-owned and -operated shop

with a wide range of ingredients. Vegan vegetable bouillon, sea salt, skillet spray, egg replacer mix, vegan chocolate drops, and much more. At the time of this publication, ordering this company's products is possible by contacting 740.935.3146 or on the Internet, see <www.differentdaisy.com>

Edensoy: Soy milk with broad availability in the United States.

Ener-G: Makes a popular vegan egg substitute as well as wheat-free, gluten-free sliced bread, available at some groceries and many health food shops. You can also order it from the vegan-owned shop *A Different Daisy* via the Internet at <www.differentdaisy.com>. Also see *Ener-G bread* and *Egg Replacers* in the previous section's *Key to Ingredients, Nutrients, and Vegetarian Terms.*

Florida Crystals natural sugar: There is no animal bone char or any other animal by product used in the manufacturing of Florida Crystals, a sugar produced by the Florida Crystals Corporation of West Palm Beach, Florida. No additives, preservatives, or artificial ingredients are added. Internet ordering is possible, through <http://www.floridacrystals.com/>. The customer service hotline is 877.835.2828.

Nasoya: Tofu specialists. Producers of *VitaSoy* (soy milk), *Nayonaise* (vegan mayonnaise), and *Nasoya tofu.* On the Internet, see <www.nasoya.com/nasoya>.

Nature's First Law: This vegan-friendly, San Diego-based distributor advertises shredded coconut from Mexico that is cultivated by certified organic Mexican farmers. Phone them at 1.888.RAW-FOOD (1.888.729.3663). <www.sunfood.com>.

Nayonaise: See Nasoya. On the Internet, see <www.nasoya.com>.

Nutritional yeast: Nutritional yeast (saccharomyces cerevisiae) is a pleasant-tasting food yeast, grown on a molasses solution, that comes in powder or flakes. Red Star T-6635+ nutritional yeast is considered the most reliable for providing *vitamin B-12.*

Rawganique.com: Purveyors of raw, organic almond butter, tahini, and Nama Shoyu. Obviously an on-line experience, but available by the good, old-fashioned telephone as well; call toll free 1.866.335.0050 or 1.877.729.4367. Rawganique.com charges a flat-rate shipping fee of $5 per order to any address in the United States or Canada; this shipping option may take 2 to 4 weeks; ground and express shipments are faster.

Tofutti: Tofutti Brands, Inc. produces soy-based products for health food shops. All products are free of cholesterol, lactose and dairy derivatives. The company is based in New Jersey and can be reached at 908.272.2400.

Tropical Source: Company using "dedicated" machinery for vegan chocolate (no dairy traces). The company also puts effort into informing consumers that chocolate used in their product is purchased only from farms where farmers and workers are treated well. 10-ounce packages of dark chocolate "semi-sweet chips" sold at grocers with vegetarian products or health food shops.

Vitasoy: Makes a non-GMO packaged tofu with reliable texture and quality. For information, phone 1.800.848.2769 or see <http://www.vitasoy-usa.com/ethnic/>.

The "where to buy" contact information for both Canada and the United States appears at http://www.vitasoy-usa.com/ethnic/where.html.

Westbrae Natural: Owned by the Hain Celestial Group, the Westbrae brand offers mellow white miso from cultured white rice, organically grown whole soybeans, water, sea salt. Find the products at your local health food shop, or use their store locator via the Internet at <www.westbrae.com>.

White Wave: Makes "Silk" soy milks, creamers, and egg nogs. Since May of 2002, the White Wave line has been owned by Dean Foods, a large dairy company that operates more than 120 plants in the United States and Spain.

C. Suggested Cooking Equipment

Baking sheets: Insulated baking sheets. More expensive, and worth it. Essential for even baking of cookies.

Blender: An electric version is useful for preparing salad dressings, creaming tofu and much more. Immersion hand blenders are wonderfully efficient for blending soups and other hot liquids.

Cookie sheets: See *baking sheets.*

Cutting board: Wood is indispensable. Avoid plastic or synthetic cutting boards. Harmful bacteria build up in the cuts made into them over time. Wood, on the other hand, retains natural oils – even after years and years – that suppress the harmful bacteria.

Food processor: Invest in a good 3-quart capacity food processor.

Garlic press: Convenient garlic presses, built to mash one clove, are the size of a small nut-cracker and can be held in the hand.

Juicer: All of our juicing has been done with excellent results using the Juice Fountain, a fast and powerful centrifugal juicer. The Juice Fountain, which won design awards in Australia, was imported into North America by Hamilton Beach, but now only Breville is selling this model.

Measuring cups: Dry-ingredient cups nest inside each other for convenient storage. They are essential for measuring flour and sugar when baking. Spoon the ingredient into the cup and level off with a straight edge.

Measuring pitcher: A four-cup measuring pitcher (Pyrex or glass) is useful. Other smaller liquid measuring cups are necessary.

Measuring spoons: Essential. Level off the dry ingredients in measuring spoons.

Mixer: Hand-held and heavy-duty stationary electric varieties are useful for mixing cake batters, beating mashed potatoes, and for many other recipes.

Mixing bowl: It's good to have at least one large mixing bowl with a portion of its rim shaped for pouring and a portion curled for easy gripping.

Pans: With pans and pots, the general rule is that you get what you pay for, so a good set is worth having. Cast-iron pans transfer the heat more or less evenly to the ingredients being cooked, fried, steamed, or sautéed. The iron itself also plays a dietary role, as traces of it pass into the food. Iron pans require a light coating of oil after each use.

Le Creuset makes really good enamel-coated, cast iron pans – great for transferring heat and for slow cooking. Stainless steel pans, saucepans, and lids should be heavy. The copper-bottom pans are popular, for good reason, although some companies (Image, for example) make really heavy-bottom, all-steel pans that are better. Different sizes of lids are essential for covering pans on the stove when needed.

Pressure cooker: A time-saver that also saves nutrients.

Spatulas: Rubber spatulas are essential for getting every last bit of batter out of a bowl and food out of a pan.

Steaming baskets: An alternative to boiling vegetables is to gently crisp them by steaming. This preserves vital nutrients. See antioxidants in our Glossary under Key to Ingredients, Nutrients, and Vegetarian Terms. The steaming basket fits into various pans.

Whisk: A stirrer made of loops, recommended for light mixing.

Wooden spoons: Melt-proof stirring utensils. One can never have too many wooden spoons and spatulas for stirring and mixing foods being prepared over the stove.

Zester: A grater for zesting lemons, limes and oranges.

Published in the United States by

Friends of Animals

Nectar Bat Press
777 Post Road, Suite 205
Darien, Connecticut U.S. 06820

Phone: 203.656.1522
Fax: 203.656.0267
Internet: www.friendsofanimals.org

Index